My Stagedoor Family

A Multi-Genre Tribute

Lori J. Mann

www.stagedoorbooks.com

The events described in the following pages are all true. The names of some of the characters and places have been changed.

Visit
www.stagedoorbooks.com
for more information.

To my beloved Aunt Kay – you are missed to the depths. None of us will ever forget the legacy by which you lived or the dreams you had. They will live on forever through each one of us, as will you.

This book is dedicated to Gram and Gramp – Jack and Jean Mann. Without you both, our family wouldn't exist and neither would these stories. I am honored to be your last grandchild, and I thank you both for being such positive forces in my life and for supporting me always.

ACKNOWLEDGEMENTS

Thank you Mom, Dad, and Robin for never giving up on me. I depended on each of you to see me through this process and when I felt like letting go, the three of you just held on tighter. I thank my brother Mark, my sister-in-law Staci, and the rest of my family for their continued interest and support in this project. Thank you Kristin S. L. Fetterolf, editor and web designer & developer, for your expert feedback and enthusiasm. Thank you Tara L. Geserick, cover designer, for your talent and expertise. Thank you Dr. Deena R. Levy, grammarian extraordinaire, for your timely and informed responses to my many questions. Special thanks to author David Collison for granting me permission to use parts of his research to help me with mine. I am sincerely grateful to all of you for seeing something in my writing and for having the confidence in me to carry it through. Thank you, each and every one of you, for being a part of this exciting journey. I would not have done it without you.

CONTENTS

Gram and Gramp on an afternoon date in 1939.

My Stagedoor Family

A Multi-Genre Tribute

PREFACE

~

The following pages tell the story of my family's New Hampshire summer cottage, Stagedoor, which my paternal grandfather helped build during the Great Depression. When I began writing this book, I intended to focus on the history of my grandparents and the intergenerational stories within our family, all of which would be written during my summer vacations at Stagedoor Camp.

I made the decision to write this book because four years ago, when I was twenty-six years old, I realized that I didn't know my grandparents as intimately as I always thought I did. I began to learn a lot about them as working people in the theatre, and I was immediately fascinated by

Gramp's pioneering work in the field of sound design on Broadway. In attempt to recreate their stories in written form, I conducted extensive interviews which have enabled me to tell them here with the utmost accuracy.

My Stagedoor Family is a multi-genre piece consisting, in part, of oral history, memoir of place, personal memoir, and stream of consciousness. I believe the latter is the most accurate representation of my voice, as stream of consciousness is wholly indicative of how I express myself in spoken language.

Though these stories were born over the course of several generations, *My Stagedoor Family* was written from 2007 to 2010. In its initial form, this book was my thesis project in graduate school. After defending my thesis and obtaining my Master's degree in Writing, I decided that I needed time to create a distance between the stories and myself. I vowed to come back to it when I was ready. After fifteen months, I was.

I have taken my profound interest in my grandparents' accounts and combined it with my passion for writing, hence preserving the legacy of our special place in the mountains for the generations to come.

PROLOGUE
Stars

~

Growing up, my paternal grandparents lived in Hillsdale, New Jersey, which was about a two-hour drive from where we lived. As a young girl, it seemed like they were always around. They never missed a holiday. I was a competitive gymnast, my brother Mark was involved in various sports, and, as I remember, they never missed a competition or a game. I remember all the times Mark and I stared out the window or played outside while we waited for their Oldsmobile station wagon to turn the corner. Once parked, Gramp would get out and walk around to the passenger side to open the door for Gram and they would walk toward us, hand-in-hand and all smiles. They have always been a constant, wholesome presence in my life.

In the last few years, I started to learn about who my grandparents were before they were grandparents. I've learned about what kind of children they were, the circumstances in which they grew up, how their parents raised them, and how they spent their working lives contributing to the society they were a part of. Through learning all of this, I also learned just how modest they both are. While their modesty is an admirable characteristic of them individually, I couldn't help but feel a bit harried when I realized how unaware I was made to be all these years, when it came to their work in the theatre. I chose not to focus on that, though, and instead I focused on the situation as it stood: Gram and Gramp were still alive and alert, which meant the stories were still able to be told by them. Simply put, they were interested and available, and I was primed and determined. I didn't want to just know their story; I wanted to write it. I wanted to write it so anyone who wanted to know about them and didn't, could.

Initially, I wanted to write this for my Gram and Gramp. After giving it some thought, however, I decided not to write it for them because they already know the stories more intimately than any of us. They don't need to be told how special Stagedoor Camp is, how much they are admired and adored, or how deeply our cottage in the woods affects and has affected all of whom have come to experience it during the last seventy-two years. Gram and Gramp know the stories. They have lived them. They began creating them long before any of us was brought to this Earth. They are the story, and so it doesn't need to be told to them.

Their story, then, shall be documented for our children – Cousin Tara's, Cousin Bob's, Mark's and mine. It is for those who have come, or who will come to us, toward the latter part of our eldest generations' lives. Of course they will grow up hearing the same stories. They will learn to walk on the porch at Camp and to ski on the lake, just as we all did before them. But aside from Jack and Kevin, who are the oldest of the great-grandchildren at twelve and nine years old, respectively, by the time they are old enough to understand their own human capacity and abilities, to have memories of their own, and relationships with the people who collectively make up those memories, two of the most influential people in all of our lives will not be inasmuch the characters they are today – the characters by whom we have been blessed, with whom we have grown and learned, by whom we have been advised, on whom we have counted, and for whom we have prayed.

And so this story must be brought to life for all of our children, especially those who will miss knowing these two extraordinary people in their lifetime. For all of our children, I write.

To Jack Christopher:

I was nineteen years old when you were born and I was a bit of a lost soul. I worked to save and lived to travel; I was the lone gypsy child floating from one part of the world to the next. I wanted to be tied to nothing. I was all about the experience. But I couldn't wait to meet you. On August 9, 1998, when you were thirty-six days old, I finally did. It was a Sunday. I watched your mom carry you from the car toward me, and when she reached the deck outside your Grammie and Pa's house, she handed you to me. You were a tiny bundle wrapped in white, and as I wrote to you that night, the moment I first looked at you, I imagined your heart, so tiny, yet so powerful. And mine, so suddenly capable of a love I never knew existed. In the last twelve years, you have grown from that baby boy into a spectacular pre-teen. You will always have a place in my heart that no one else could ever fill.

To Kevin Charlie:

When I found out that your mom was pregnant with you, I was scared. I wondered how I could possibly love another child as much as I already loved your brother. Where would the love come from? Then I looked at you. And there it was.

In July 2005, you were four years old. I drove to your house on my way home from New Hampshire to spend a few days with you and Jack. You asked if you could go with me on "an adventure" and spend a couple of days at my house, so I brought you home with me. Do you remember? That first night with you, I didn't sleep. Instead, I watched you sleep and I wrote this:

Kevin Charlie,
Talk all day, I will listen.
Play anytime and I'll watch.
Sleep all night; I lie awake.
Your existence is reassuring to all that I once doubted.
There is a force greater than all of us.
Sweet child of excellence, you blow me away.
Young child of wonder - from you I learn so much.
You are a wunderkind - supremely wrapped and delivered...
A precise creation of all things magnificent.
Kevin Charlie, my heart screams your name.
You are a golden opportunity - another life to love.
Let me be a part of you forever.
Honor me with that.
Delicate and brilliant, you are a masterpiece.

To Benjamin Robert:

And the love swept over me again. The moment I learned your mom was pregnant with you, I loved you. I knew that I would love you even more by the time I met you. When I looked at you, I felt a familiarity with your soul. My love for you was immediate and profound. You are a joy, beautiful boy, in my life and a blessing in my heart. I love watching you grow and explore your world. When you smile, I don't blink; when you laugh, I nearly cry. You whisper delight with every breath. You are a ray of sunshine. I haven't seen nearly enough of you in your two years since birth, but I look forward to loving you for the rest of my life.

To Brady Cullen:

By the time I learned that your mom was pregnant with you, I knew better than to wonder where the love would come from. You were one more life to love and I knew just how I would love you. You were one more spot in my heart – a place that I never realized was empty until I knew it would be filled by you. And for that, I was eager to meet you. It's been five hundred forty seven days since my heart was transformed again.

To the Mann child(ren):

Child(ren) of my brother's seed, how I love you so. I have thought of you for many years. I dream of getting word that you are on your way to us. Your Mommy and Daddy will be such wonderful parents. You will grow up happy, having been born to them and into a close family who will shower you with love always. It will be an honor to love you and to show you many things. As your aunt, it will be my duty and my pleasure. Until you grace us with your presence, I will continue to love the idea of loving you in person.

To my child(ren):

Dearest star(s) in the sky,
I ache to hold, touch, kiss, and smell you at this moment. I lie on the porch, iPod in ears, rainstorm outside. I have taken my glasses off and can barely see the page onto which my heart is bleeding. Another year has come and gone. I have smiled a year's worth of smiles, cried a year's worth of tears. I look out at the lake and I am overcome

with a sense of wonderment. I am five months from twenty-nine and a long way from you. My womb…barren, aching, for years felt lonely and depressed. I prayed not to a god, but to it – my womb of spongy pinkness, thirsty for life to greet it. Sometimes I fear that I have wished too much for you. That I spent too many years living for the future -- when you were here with me -- and not enough time in the present. I don't know if I will meet you in this life or the next, but my hopes and dreams for and of you remain.

Child(ren), everyday I am blown away by how much I love you…by how desperately I can miss you – you whom I have not yet held, touched, kissed or smelled. You have not yet been created, and it scares me how much I already love you. There are many things I want to do for you and with you. The books I've already bought for you. The one I'm writing for you. I will not feel whole until I have held you. Touched you. Kissed you. Smelled you.

To all of our children, present and future, let me introduce you to your great-grandparents – the staples of our special Camp, Stagedoor. Your great-grandfather was born Jack Robert Mann in 1923. He is "Gramp" to you and to mostly all who know him closely. He is a kind, gentle soul. If you could truly know him, my sweet loves, you would know a man of impatience, much like his four grandchildren, who exist, in part, to learn and share his wisdom. He is a simple man with simple desires. His final wish in this life is to have a great-grandson to carry on his surname. You'd quickly penetrate his outer shell and see how easy he is to figure out. He loves you with every ounce of his being, but he might never tell you. He doesn't have to. You'd occasionally become frustrated by his dry sense of humor, but once you understood him, it would only make you love him more. What you just might love the most about him is the way he looks at your great-grandmother.

Her name is Jean, but to us and to you she is "Gram." She is one year older than Gramp, and she is tall and beautiful and wants so desperately to know each and every one of you. She adores you, Jack, Kevin, Ben, Brady, and she can't wait to get her hands on the rest of you who are yet to come. None of us can.

Gramp looks at Gram with such devotion...afraid to blink for fear of missing seeing her glance back at him. She smiles at him with her eyes, not just her mouth. His name alone makes her visibly lighter, and the sight of her always stops him in his tracks. He'd tell you that she is his most prized possession, then he'd add "If you can call her a possession." Lately, he sometimes looks at her with a certain hesitation...it's in his eyes...as if with every moment, he's sending a plea out into the universe. He sometimes looks at her with a certain fear…the fear of ever having to live without her. Kids, he couldn't.

Know that if you ever saw a couple in love, they would be your great-grandparents.

And so the story begins.

To all of you kids: I love you each.

CHAPTER 1
The Grand Tour of Stagedoor

~

Grandparents fascinate me. They have so many stories to tell. If mine could live to be a hundred and fifty years old, there'd still be so much I wouldn't know about them. I've never tried so hard to hold on to every breath, every glance, every hug, every kiss…every story, every home-cooked meal, every smile and every laugh - every second we spend together.

When Gram and Gramp retired in 1986, they started spending every May to October at Camp. The last few years, though, they've only gone up from June to the beginning of September because they decided the trip was too long for them to make alone. Unfortunately once they began needing the family to help get them there, open

Camp, and drive them home in the fall, they weren't able to stay quite as long as they were used to.

When they're in New Jersey, we have monthly sleepovers. I call them "Grandparents Days." I drive to their house in the afternoon and we spend the day together catching up. I bring hoagies from our favorite sub shop on the White Horse Pike and when we get hungry again, we normally go to dinner at our favorite restaurant, JR's, in Absecon. After dinner, we go back to their house and talk some more. Nowadays Gramp goes to sleep between nine-thirty and ten o'clock, but when I visit, he often stays up until close to eleven. After he goes to bed, Gram and I talk for several more hours.

I have always seemed to miss them so much more after spending time with them. I sometimes hide Post-It notes all over their house for them to find after I leave. On them, I write messages like, *Who loves you?* (something my dad has always said to me), *I will miss you until I see you again*, and, *Smile — you are loved!* I hide them in their utensil drawers and under their pillows. I tape them to their ceiling fan, and they tell me they're still finding them two and three days after I've been there.

Lately, though, I miss them even when I am with them. After Gram and I say goodnight, I walk past their bedroom and blow a kiss to Gramp, asleep in their bed. I whisper, "Goodnight again, Gramp. Rest well this night. I love you." I secretly wish they could both live forever, but I don't tell them that because I know they wouldn't want to. When I go to sleep at night, I miss them...and I know I'll see them in the morning.

Though Gram and Gramp have each other, I imagine they must feel lonely at times. When you've spent close to seventy years with someone, there isn't anything they don't know about you. I wonder how it feels to have a person in your life who knows *everything* about you not because you've told them all of your stories, but because they experienced each of them with you. And so they spend a good part of their days talking about family, friends, doctors' appointments, what's going on in the world, music, movies, and television. They look forward to family gatherings. In fact, they probably, at this point in their lives, live for such times. *So do we.*

Some of my best thinking takes place while I'm driving. My mind can slow down and my thoughts run free. As a freelance Sign Language Interpreter, I spend a lot of time in my car making my way from one job to the next. My thoughts usually go straight to my family because I often talk to them while I drive - when I have a few minutes between Point A and Destination B. While I listen to the phone ring, sometimes I think about the person I'm calling. I try to imagine them in their setting. I wonder, are they a five-minute walk from me? A day's drive? A plane ride? What were they doing before their phone rang? Are they as happy to hear from me as I am to call them?

Likewise, sometimes I do not think about the person I'm calling. I just go through the motions while I drive. I don't like for more than a few days to go by without checking in with those closest to me. I always have a list of calls to make, but I usually only have about fifteen minutes to talk. I dial the number without even looking down from the road. I listen to the *ring, ring, ring* and I think about everything and sometimes nothing. It is almost as if I am in a hypnotic state – deeply relaxed, but aware of my surroundings. And sometimes, when I hear the person pick up on the other end of the line, I forget whom I called altogether.

Today is a typical summer day in New Jersey. The humidity has exhausted me. I try to stay indoors when the heat is this intense. I like to sweat, but not while my hair is still wet from the shower. I hate this time of year in New Jersey. Another year has come and gone, and in a few days, I'll be driving back to the mountains at last to spend the month with Gram and Gramp at Stagedoor. I have to pick up some snacks for the road, a bottle of sunscreen and a few other last-minute items for my trip. While I drive with the air conditioner on full blast, my thoughts drift to Gram and Gramp sitting outside our cottage in the late-afternoon New England summer breeze. Suddenly, I can hear the sounds of the lake getting rough and I can smell the fresh

Camp air. This experience wouldn't be complete without the sounds of their voices.

"Hel-lo," Gramp says, in his robotic manner of answering the telephone.

"Hey, Gramp! What are you up to?"

"Hiya, Sis! Mother and I are sittin' out here under the tree looking at the lake. We were wondering when we were gonna hear from the little girl. How's the schoolhouse?" I'm the youngest of the four grandchildren on my father's side of the family and the only perpetual student. I have never yet had a conversation with Gramp without him asking about "the schoolhouse." He is a man of few words, but he is full of pride for each of his grandchildren. Tara is a massage therapist; Bob is a commercial diver; Mark owns a custom cage business and breeds exotic birds. Gramp has a way of making each of us feel special…without trying.

"School is good. It's a lot of work, but I'm not complaining. Work's great, too! It's been another really busy week."

"Good," he says, "tell Mom about it." With that, he passes the phone to Gram, whom he affectionately refers to as "Mom."

"Hell-oo," she answers, emphasizing the second syllable of the word, unlike Gramp's emphasis of the first. Her voice sounds sweet to my ears and is always full of interest. My heart smiles.

"Hi, Gram," I say with a particular excitement in my voice that I only hear when it calls to her.

"Well, hello, Lori," she says with her trademark giggle. I can feel her love every time I speak with her, whether I am standing in front of her with arms outstretched, or she is sitting under the tree at Camp - a day's drive from where I happen to be. "So what's new? Gramp and I were just wondering when we'd hear from you."

"Aw...you're so funny. I never go more than a few days without calling you! But I'm great! How are you? I can't wait to see you in a few more days. I miss you both so much!"

She giggles and says, "Oh? Well, we miss you, too, Lori." I can almost hear her smile. "We're just fine! When will you be here?"

"I'll be leaving on Monday morning at around three o'clock or so. I should be there by lunchtime."

"Oh," she giggles, "good. Well now, you just take your time and we'll see you when you get here. We're looking forward to hearing all about school and everything else that's been going on in your life. We had a wonderful visit with Tara and the boys. We'll tell you all about it when you get here. You be careful now."

"Thanks, Gram. I will be. I'll call you when I get to Sturbridge. I love you. I can't wait to see you!"

"We love you, too, Sweetheart. Bye."

A few short days later, my alarm sounds, but I am already awake. I can never sleep the night before I leave for Camp. It's like the kid who gets a good night's sleep on Christmas Eve. Who does that?

I'm in the truck, on my way to the New Jersey Turnpike by 3:30 am. If I don't get through New York by rush hour, I wind up going through Hartford at lunchtime. Then it takes me twelve hours to get there. Leaving this early only takes eight or nine. *Only. It's a hell of a drive by yourself.* I listen to CD after CD and I drive hour after hour. I always stop off in Sturbridge, Massachusetts, to fill up my gas tank. That's when I call Gram and Gramp to tell them I'm about halfway there. This is also when I tend to start speeding. The closer I get to New Hampshire (and to them), the faster I drive.

At long last, I turn onto the dirt road leading to our Camp. It actually has a name, but to my family, it will always be "the Dirt Road" because it hadn't yet been given a name in 1938 when the cabin was built. The narrow, winding dirt road looked much like a trail. For many years, it was so narrow, in fact, that drivers actually had to pull off the road to allow oncoming vehicles to pass. The windows are down in my truck and I inhale slowly and as deeply as my lungs permit – taking in the cleanliness and all the beauty of the mountains, the trails, the cottages, the trees, the rocks, the lake, and, at last, when I make the final turn, the family cottage, Stagedoor.

My favorite moment of the entire year is this one – when I turn onto our property and see our cottage and Gram and Gramp's station wagon. I have experienced this moment every summer of my life, and the feelings become more intense with each year.

Every year, unless it happens to be raining, when I pull onto our property, Gram is outside in her garden, picking off the dried petals from her flowers and throwing them into the woods. Before I can even get out of my truck, Gramp comes out of the house and waits for me to open the door of my truck. Hugs and kisses are exchanged and while Gramp carries my suitcase inside, Gram and I act like two schoolgirls bursting with excitement because we are finally together again.

"Come on in," Gram says, "I've fixed you some lunch."

After lunch, I begin the next Camp ritual – saying hello to Camp itself. I do the same thing every year, carefully following the same order. I have done this for as long as my memory serves. I walk through the entire Camp, without speaking. This is always a particularly emotional time for me for several reasons. First, because I am back at Stagedoor again – something I have thought about and longed for every day since the day I left the year before. Second, because I am, at last, back in the presence of Gram and Gramp – whom I have missed greatly in the previous two or three months since they left their home in New Jersey to come up here. And third, because I have an overwhelming awareness of my ancestors' presence not just within the confines of Stagedoor, but in the air that I breathe…the sweet New England air.

I start by the back door. For the most part, everyone enters and exits through this door. Because Stagedoor is lakefront property, the grass driveway leads to the back of the house. When I walk through the door, I am in the kitchen. The bathroom is on the right. Turning left, walking through the kitchen, I reach the main part of the cottage. Through the portal, I look to the left at the dining nook. I glance at the pictures on the walls of the cottage before turning my body to the right where I drag my fingers across the back support of the couch and walk through the cottage. I pass both bedrooms on my left, and I end up standing in the doorway of the porch.

The porch is my favorite part of the inside of Camp. This is where the kids always sleep. All of my New England summer thunderstorm memories were made here. Robin, my other mother, always lightly sandwiched my head between two pillows on her lap and spoke to me in her comforting voice. She kept me safe this way until the crackling thunder stopped.

I look to the left – my side of the porch, as opposed to the right which was Mark's side growing up. I wonder which sides cousins Tara and Bob slept on when they were kids. Our families always had separate vacations up here. It wasn't until Tara's boys, Jack and Kevin, were born that I sometimes came up during their holiday.

I wonder if it's possible to count the number of mornings my dad came in and woke me with the soothing touch of his hand across the side of my face. "Morning, Lor," he'd say. "It's time to go skiing." The porch, facing the lake, is enclosed by sixteen large, screened windows, so I'd open my eyes and there would be the lake - flat and shiny as glass. Mark and I would jump out of bed and into our swim suits before Dad even got down to the dock. Out on the lake, when it was my turn to ski, I'd jump into the water - so cold it would temporarily numb my whole body. By the next morning, I'd forget how cold the water was, and after Dad came in to wake us and we were out on the lake, I'd jump in and experience the same shock. Morning after morning, year after year.

I turn away from the lake and look at the furniture on the porch. The dresser on the right has four drawers, whereas the one on the left only has three. I imagine that was the determining factor, once upon a time, for who would stay on which side. I always wanted the extra drawer. I wonder if Tara did, too. I believe those dressers are the same dressers that have been up here since before we grandchildren were born. I put my purse on top of the dresser and sit on the futon, facing Mark's side of the porch. This is where each of us kids slept every summer…forever…and we still do. Dad and Aunt Kay slept here when they were kids. Gramp slept here when he was a kid. Four generations have enjoyed this place since Eddie built it. Jack, Kevin, Ben, and Brady are the fifth generation to meet Camp.

Gramp walks onto the porch. His hands are folded in front of him and he's looking out at the lake. He must know exactly what I'm thinking. *Of course he does.* "People who don't know us probably think this place is pretty strange," he says. "They don't understand the motive. Camp is for the kids. They learn to walk right here on this porch and it just goes on from there." We all learned to walk on this porch, and, turning to look outside again, I think about how we also all learned to ski on this lake.

Gram always makes her corn chowder, a family favorite, for dinner on the evening any of us arrives because, as she says "…it's a quick meal and that way we can get right to catching up." After we're all filled in on the goings-on in one another's lives, the conversation usually turns to Gramp's work in the theatre. Tonight, though, as I looked around Camp, I wanted to know where and how all of this began. Gramp's parents were from Michigan.

Michigan is a fourteen-hour drive from here. What brought them here? How did they even meet?

CHAPTER 2
The Trunk That Went *Kerplunk*

~

"The name of the show was *By the Sea*. The A.B. Marcus Show traveled across the country for twenty-eight weeks from September 1920 to April 1921. It changed names in '21 and the name escapes me, but it isn't important. It was a revue with a bunch of girls and a bunch of comics – something that came along during the era of Vaudeville. It was during that show, in 1921, that Dad met Mother."

Gramp's thin lips stretch into a wide and even thinner smile. I push the weight of my body up with my arms and swing my legs underneath me, sitting Indian-style on the blue upholstered couch in the main part of the cottage. We have just moved from the table to the couch, where we can sit more comfortably. When I'm up here, Gram and I take turns cooking dinner and cleaning up. When I cook she cleans up and on the nights when she cooks, I clean up. Tonight, though, she cooked and cleaned up. She never lets me do either on the day that I arrive.

The yellow bug light from the lamp behind me casts a soft warmth across Gramp's face. We are sitting by the fireplace and he is telling me the story of how his parents met. Leaning closer to him, I try not to blink. I don't want to miss anything.

Gramp tips his head back and looks slightly upward. He is recalling a distant memory. With each exhale, he pulls the story closer to the present, until the reminiscent air about his face has faded, and he begins recounting the story as though it happened last week.

"So when you move a show from one town to another, you have wagons that pick the show up at the theatre and horses that drive the wagons to the railroad station. You unload all the stuff into a railroad car. And they always used baggage cars. If you bought so many tickets, you got the baggage car free. The Marcus Show was big enough that you could buy enough passenger tickets, so the baggage car didn't cost you anything. So the railroad, having to give you the baggage car, would give you the worst one they had that was made specifically to haul horses. It was full of stalls! Well, you can imagine the stagehand who gets to his baggage car that night after the show is over. He's got to load all his stuff in this car, and of course you can't put anything in it. It's full of stalls. You have to take all the stalls out. They're portable. The old guys used to scream and holler about that."

Gramp is my favorite storyteller. When he tells stories about his past, he talks with such emotion, such passion. His face brightens and, immediately, his entire being appears ten years younger. I often have to remind myself to pay attention when he talks, not for lack of interest, but for concentration overload.

"Years later, the baggage cars that I loaded were horse baggage cars," he continues. "But all the stalls had been taken out. So civilization helped a little bit." This flash forward in time slightly disturbs the flow of the story for me and I have discovered where that comes from in my own storytelling.

"So, Dad is loading the stuff. Part of the show stuff is trunks that belong to each member of the cast. My mother is in the chorus group, she's a showgirl you see, and she had this trunk with her name on it - Etta Wray. Well, the trunk had been dropped a few times and was all tied together with clothesline rope. Dad is unloading it this particular day, shoving trunks from the truck into the baggage car, when *kerplunk!*, her trunk falls on its side, opens up, and stuff falls out everywhere! Dad is fit to be tied. He gathers up the junk, sees whose name is on it and when he sees her later, tells her 'Ma'am, get your trunk fixed.'"

"'You're so smart, why don't you fix it?'" she said.

"HA!" he chuckles, looking at me and shaking his head. "And that was Mother."

"So did he fix it?" I ask.

"Did he fix it? Out in the shop is a little, tiny red-handled hammer -- very small -- called a riveting hammer," he points toward the shed outside by our cottage. That's the hammer my father repaired her trunk with. Everybody wonders why I want to keep track of that hammer! I've got four tack hammers out there and everybody grabs my little red one. So I gotta take it home this trip. It should not stay up here."

Gram just finished cleaning up from dinner and has joined us in the living room. She sits down on the rocking chair next to the fireplace and, with a smile, takes off her white canvas shoes. Once settled in the chair, she rests her long, straight back on the back support of the chair and begins to rock. She is, in all her years of beauty, the most polished woman I know.

"So what exactly did Eddie do?" Edward was my great-grandfather's name, but he was always known as Eddie. "I know he did more than toss suitcases into the stalls of trains after the shows."

"Oh, boy!" Gramp agrees. "In 1917, he went to Flint and became the electrician of a beautiful, brand-new theatre, the Palace Theatre. He was sponsored by a fellow in Battle Creek, Selby Collins, who'd been there for a hundred years. Before 1917, he was an usher at the Bijou Theatre in Michigan. Selby sent him to Flint. 'As of now, you're an electrician!'" he says pretending to be Selby.

"He then went on to work as a stagehand at the Capitol Theatre in Michigan. He worked as a flyman. People who don't know about the theatre don't know what a flyman is. The scenery that you looked at for the most part in 1920 was a backdrop and there were a few things in front of the backdrop to give it a little bit of depth. The flyman, in Dad's case, had thirty-five flats to worry about. It's got to have ropes and pulleys and stuff for each one. So they had a bracket where you could roll a drop up and hook it with three brackets and use the drop that's in the front for the opening act."

"At intermission," he continues, "the stage crew goes out there and rolls up the other drop you have used already, flips the other one out, and puts this one in the three hooks. So in a fifteen to twenty minute intermission, you could hang up, or expose, ten more drops. So my father was a flyman. He went to Flint with nothing but a job. He worked there from 1917 to 1960 when he retired. He died that year, too."

"What kind of man was he?"

"He was a smart man, but he only got to the eighth grade in the schoolhouse. He was quite impatient, I think because he was so smart. He was serious but he had a great sense of humor at the same time. And he was always smiling."

I never met Eddie. Everyone in Gramp's family died young. According to Gramp, he himself has been on "borrowed time" since his early seventies. Gramp is getting tired in this life. I drop my head and focus my attention on my fingernails that I've been picking. I hate that I have this habit, and I'm trying to break it. I fold my hands on my lap and wonder what I'll ask Gramp next. I need to ask him as many questions as I can while I still have him here. There is so much to know.

I decide that I'll ask about my great-grandmother, Etta Wray, because I don't know much about her either. All I know about her is that she sounds like she could have been a bit sassy when she was young and that she was a showgirl...I'm not even sure what that is exactly. A picture of her hangs on the wall in the hallway of Gram and Gramp's house in New Jersey. Parts of it have been painted, to bring color to the antique photograph. I have spent enough time looking at that photograph that I can see her clearly when I close my eyes. She is tall and elegant in her Queen of Hearts costume. She holds her arms out gracefully to the sides and looks at the camera, with a gentle smile. Her dark hair is cut to just below her ears. Her skin is fair and she has large, round eyes that are placed wide on her face and deeply set. Though it is difficult to discern the exact color of her eyes from this photograph, they do not appear dark. Since no one in my father's family has dark eyes, I conclude that hers must be light. Her Irish features are strong. She was striking and I can't help but remark on what a resemblance Aunt Kay bears to her.

Clearly a star in her day, I want very much to learn about her. I want to know about her as a person, not just a renowned American beauty. I wonder what kind of mother she was to my Gramp and what kind of great-grandmother she might have been to me.

"What do you miss most about her?"

"Her smile," he says without hesitation. "She was a happy lady. Quiet, but happy."

"Where was she born?"

"Haverhill, Massachusetts. 1898. I don't know anything about her." The glimmer in his eyes turns wistful, cueing me to ask another question.

"Do you know how she became a showgirl?" I can feel my heart in my chest. A tiny belt is wrapped around it just a little too tight. I have never met this woman, but by merely talking about her, I can feel her presence in the room, and I am nervous. I have so many questions for her…questions about her life and her work. Questions about my Gramp when he was a boy. He's an only child and since all of his relatives are deceased, his stories from his memory of his childhood are the only stories I will ever know. I depend on the accuracy of his memory to learn as much about my great-grandmother as I can.

"I suppose I know some stuff about Mother," he decides. "But not much. Listen carefully and I'll tell you everything I know." He looks up at me through his big hazel eyes and I think. *Wow, they resemble his mother's.* I adjust my position on the couch, grabbing the blanket from the chair next to me, and I watch Gramp with curious intent as though I were watching a Broadway show.

"She had a sister nine years older than her. She came from a Catholic family. She was sort of a rebel. She and a girlfriend joined a girls' show called the A.B. Marcus Show. There are three kinds of girls in the chorus -- they have the nickname of ponies, mediums, or showgirls. Showgirls are always the tallest and they wear the ultra-fancy costumes and they pose in the back of the stage because the girls in a partially undressed form can't move -- they gotta stand still. So the curtain opens to show you a scene, the medium dance girls would be there dancing and the ponies are the little ones out front. You haven't even seen the showgirls yet. There's a piece of scenery in the way. So.....you invent the rest of the picture. Everything was a picture -- no movement at the time of exposing the girls."

I can picture the stage and hear the music. I can visualize the ultra-fancy costumes and the scenery. I look through Gramp's eyes as he speaks to me and I can see my great-grandmother, *Etta Wray: Showgirl*.

"Dad was from Michigan and Mother, I just told you, was from Massachusetts, so they musta met somewhere between here and here," he points his index fingers downward, one in front of himself and the other about two feet away, closer to where I'm sitting. "I don't know how fast it happened, but it couldn't have been too long. I know they were certainly engaged in Washington, D.C. and they didn't get married until Atlantic City. Now there's a story!"

To everyone who knows Gramp, he is affectionately referred to as "a man of few words." When it comes to his family and the theatre, though, he can talk all day. He has gotten older, but he hasn't lost a bit of energy when the conversation turns to either topic. Every time we visit, we spend several hours talking. Well, he does the talking. I ask the questions and take the notes.

"So they get to Atlantic City - and the reason I know this is they got married a couple of days before Easter, maybe the day before - and the church is all decorated for Easter. Now here's the stagehand, his wife-to-be, and their best friends - a couple - people who worked in the show. So when the matinée is over they go to Saint Paul's Church and they get married. And, of course, when they see this church for the first time it takes their breath away -- it was gorgeous! Lilies and daffodils and stuff everywhere."

I wonder if the church is still there. I imagine myself alone in the church with the apparitions of my great-grandparents on their wedding day eighty-seven years ago. I envision Etta Wray in her showgirl attire, though she may have worn a traditional white dress. I'll never know.

"There's more to the wedding story, Sis. Wake up." He brings me out of my head and back to the present. I watch him closely, observing the freshness in his eyes as they appear younger before me. My face aches from the unremitting smiles he induces.

"So Dad's got this program for tomorrow's Easter services and he tucks it away and keeps it there. When he and Mother are in Lynn visiting my mother's mother, Grandma Clohecy, he shows her the program and she reads the cover, 'Saint Paul's So-and-So Church.' So Grandma Clohecy reads the 'Saint Paul's' and that's as far as she reads. She was tickled to death that they got married in a Catholic church! Guess what, Sis. They didn't! St. Paul's wasn't a Catholic Church. So we gotta find out -- Saint Paul's Church, 1921 in Atlantic City - is it Methodist or Greek or what is it? HA!"

"Her parents were religious?" I ask laughing.

"Well, religious enough to want her to get married in a Catholic Church, I guess."

"What about your parents? How were

"Short of going to church, my parents
religious. Mother took me to Christian Science Church
from the time I was this big…" he exaggerates his point by
lowering his hand to below the armrest on which his elbow
had been leaning. Gram and I glance at each other and
smile. "…until I grew up to about fourteen and then I went
to a Presbyterian Church. My parents certainly gave me a
program to follow, but they weren't strict to the point of
beating me with a club."

I am surprised to hear this because I've never
known Gram or Gramp to go to church in my lifetime. I
grew up knowing my father was raised Presbyterian and
both Mom and Robin were raised Jewish. None of our
parents are particularly religious, so Mark and I never
really went to church or synagogue. It wasn't until I grew
older when I had the desire to explore religion, but it didn't
take me long to figure out that my beliefs were not
conducive to those of any type of organized religion.
Luckily, nothing was ever forced on us. I'd have rebelled
like Etta Wray. I wonder if that's why she became a
showgirl.

Not wanting the conversation to turn toward
religion, I continue with my questions. "So you were born
the next year. What do you remember about that?" I joked.
I have a reputation of asking Gram and Gramp countless
questions. Sometimes I think I border on "annoying,"

though no one's ever accused me of being so. When I'm with Gram and Gramp, I ask one question right after the other. They tell me they are amazed at how many questions I can ask. I tell them that after asking so many questions, I am amazed at how much I still don't know.

"Well, I am the first baby to be born in a brand new hospital in Flint -- The Women's Hospital. It didn't open until two months after I was born. In their records, I'm Baby #1. April 6, 1923."

I smile at the thought of Gramp as a baby and I can't imagine how being born in a hospital before it opened is possible. Then I remind myself that he is talking about 1923, when the cost of a First-Class Stamp was two cents. A lot has changed since then.

Changing the subject back to Eddie and Etta Wray, determined to get as much information about them as I can, I say, "So when The Marcus Show ended, your mom moved to Michigan with your dad. What brought them to New Hampshire? Michigan is a fourteen hour drive from here, isn't it?"

I remember when I was a little girl, I'd always ask my mom to read me the same stories. I had them memorized, but there was something about the way she read them to me that I always felt like the ending might change or the characters might rise from the pages and come play with me. There was something magical about having those stories read to me. Here I am, more than twenty-five years later, doing the same thing with my Gramp. I already know the story of how his parents found the lake - I've heard it many times, but I want to hear Gramp tell it again. Every time he repeats a story he adds another detail. I still don't want to miss the magic.

CHAPTER 3
Building a Dream

~

"Mother's sister, my Aunt Kitty, lived on the water in Lynn, Mass, about ten miles north of Boston. She had a dear friend, Ellie Orbison, who she worked with in a shoe shop making shoes. She had to work in some shoe factory and there's nobody alive today who could tell you how many of them she worked in. But I can recall the *last* one she worked in. On the first floor of all the buildings there was more or less unused space. Like, if a fella was going to build a theatre he goes to the cheapest part of town and he buys a piece of property and converts it to a theatre because it's the cheapest piece of property in town. Shoe factories - same thing. So these gray-haired ladies would walk up three flights of stairs and do their fancy stitching.

So in 1937, Mrs. Orbison and her husband Bill invited Aunt Kitty to their cottage they had built three or four years earlier on this lake. Starting at three months old, Mother brought me to Lynn to visit my aunt every summer. In 1937, when I was fourteen, the trip included spending a weekend at the Orbison's cottage, Camp Ellie."

Gramp smiles, "I remember Mr. Orbison taking us for a ride in his big wooden boat. As soon as we got out of the car, we were in that boat. He had found a boat piled up in the sand down at the Sandy Beach that spring. He hauled it back here in three pieces. It was just a mess! He rebuilt the whole thing...fixed it all up. That's the boat he took Dad and I for a ride in that summer. 'Speed, we gotta get one of these!' Dad said. There are pictures in my album of a boat that's almost identical to the one that Bill had put together. Anyway, Father fell in love with the place immediately. While he was falling in love with the boat and the lake, Mother was inside the camp falling in love with it. So before we left to go back home, my father decided that we needed a camp and a boat of our own."

At the end of that weekend, Eddie asked Aunt Kitty if she'd look for some lots that were for sale. That winter, she found a couple of lots on the lake. "I remember her calling Dad on the telephone telling him there was one in Bryant Bay and there was one right here, a few lots down from Camp Ellie. She had three of them altogether. She was just beside herself. Kitty was a particularly neat person. She had three choices and it was almost impossible. So this is the one she picked out because there was always a breeze on the lake. The bays, in the middle of summer, are often unbearable. Everything is too still. There, ninety-one is ninety-one, but here, ninety-one is comfortable."

Aunt Kitty made the purchase and the next summer Gramp and his parents went back to the lake to build their own camp - a mirror image of Camp Ellie. Eddie and Etta Wray, both of course still working in the theatre, had two weeks' vacation. Since the drive took two days each way, they had just ten days to build the entire cottage. With the help of Etta Wray's cousin George, they built a beautiful little cottage on the lake.

"My job was to paddle the canoe back and forth between our place and Camp Ellie to make sure everyone had cold beer," Gramp says. "There wasn't much else I could do at fifteen, except hammer all the nails into the wood. After a while of doing that, you'd swear your young arms were about to fall off. Luckily by then, I had just a few more left to do until the entire camp was done. Enough to make Pop proud of young Speed," he smiles. I, too, am proud of him.

"There were a lot of things I did for this place myself. If you look behind the one by four right there --

when you are in the dinette -- you'll see the piece of wood coming this way has to be trimmed on a bevel in order to fit. Well, if you look behind there - if you sit where the toaster is and look at it - you can see that someone must have done that with a hand axe." My gaze takes me to where his outstretched arm points - back to the table where we have just eaten. "If you think about it a minute, you say, 'jeez that was done with a hand axe' because it was a fifteen-year-old kid chopping. My fingerprints are on all the roof boards up there. I had to hold 'em while I nailed them because the boards were all like this," he gestures, showing me how crooked the boards were. "This was all wet lumber that cost almost nothing. And Dad would say, 'For Christ's sake, Speed, pull on it.' And I'm just a kid, pulling on it. I'm eight to twelve feet away from him, pulling on it."

"There wasn't any electricity in '38, so every single hole you can see I put in physically with bit and brace. But when you're laying on your back under the house and trying to put two holes in where the old man wants 'em, 'What in hell are you doing down there? I want two holes!' I had just finished the first one! He was quite a taskmaster. Ya got tears in your eyes because your arm is gone. This arm is supposed to push the handle -- this big push-up. You don't spend much time pushing up in your natural life at fifteen. But it all got done. And all the holes got drilled. And we kept it going this long, so that's something."

I look around at the walls of our Camp, bedecked with autographed pictures of my family's friends from the theatre: actresses Angela Lansbury and Elizabeth Taylor; actors Joel Grey and Lex Luce (Alexis B. Luce); musicians Glenn Miller and Clyde McCoy; world class magicians Harry Blackstone and Long Tack Sam.

I look at the walls behind these photographs and I notice the boards are different widths. How could I not have noticed that before? "Why is that, Gramp?"

"Well, I'll explain it to you, Sis," he says, always eager to share information. "In the lumberyard - no lumberyard's got enough money to buy a tool for eight-inch, six-inch, and four-inch lumber. This is four over here," he points to the wall behind where he normally sits at the dinette. "That's eight," he points to the wall I lean against when I sit at the table. The dinette over *here* is six. We built the house and the kitchen cubicle in the ten-day period. The next year, 1939, we put the boards in from there to there," he says pointing first to the wall near the kitchen and then to the wall by the television. "This partition was up; it wasn't covered when we left the first year. When you go to the lumberyard to buy eight, they only sell six because that's the size tree they're cutting that year. Then the following year you want to get from that corner to this corner. That's four. 'We don't have any six-inch.' And Dad cussed them."

In the 1930s, when people built cottages, they were allowed to build as close to the water as they desired. Today, with the advent of building permits, people are not afforded this luxury. Stagedoor, a small two-bedroom lakefront cottage, sits just fifty feet from the water, while the others that were built after it sit at least one hundred feet back.

The land on which it sits, according to the deed, is "192 x 165 square feet more or less." The reason for the "more or less," is because back then, a string, as opposed to the current method of measuring, was used to divide up the land. Eddie and Etta bought two lots. The cottage sits in the middle of one lot, leaving a thick stretch of land full of trees to the right, when facing the front of the cottage.

The entire project cost five hundred dollars. Our lots were one hundred dollars each. The remaining three hundred dollars was spent on the building materials. The house, which sits on sixteen cement-filled paint cans, was, in its original size, twenty-two by twenty-eight. The first thing to be built, of course, was the "dance floor," atop the paint cans. From there, the walls and the roof were built. "The New Hampshire people told my father that the place wouldn't last two winters built like that. Here we are Sis, some seventy years later, and we're still sittin' on the same sixteen paint cans."

"1938 was still several years before the end of the Great Depression" I pointed out. "How was your family able to afford a vacation home when most of the rest of the country was experiencing intense hardship?"

"Remember the shoe shop I told you about? For a case of shoes, which was twenty pair, she'd get paid so many pennies and you would get so many cases a day for your day's pay. She made twenty-one dollars a week at the time. I'm talking about 1938, when this place was built. At the same time, my dad made fifty dollars a week. Mother's cousin, George, who helped build the place, had a job with the WPA (Works Progress Administration). Musicians in every single town in the country could go to the YMCA gymnasium and play every Friday night for people to dance and they would pay 'em. Not much, but there was a check. And several of the guys in the Capitol Theatre band took advantage of playing there to augment their income.

Alan Holmes was a flute player who played both jobs. I can think of so many of them - I can picture them, exactly who they were. Steinbach was a bass player. FDR started the WPA and that's another whole thing. You gotta give people something to do and people today can't imagine anything about the Depression time. They can't imagine. And apparently it has a pretty good chance, over the next hundred years, of happening more than once. Pretty amazing when people haven't got a job to do. Our group that works everyday, in a way, could be referred to as slaves. During the slavery time the slaves got paid by having a place to live and food to eat if they prepared it. The same thing happens today only we get money - they pay us every Friday. But the working people - not putting it in a manner of complaining - could very well be initiated this way. You would have to change the vocabulary from what it is now. *Slaves* means a certain thing. So you gotta find a new name for 'em. So they're called the working middle class. Call them anything you want; it's a group of people that is controlled by somebody else."

"In the entertainment business," he continues, "the attendance goes up in bad times. When things are the toughest, people still go to the theatre. My father was lucky because he had a job all through the Depression. In the theatre you just work twenty-six or twenty-eight weeks and you don't have a job until the next bunch of shows goes out. To get twenty-six weeks, you were a prosperous person. He started working as an usher before 1917 and he had a job until 1960. The year our camp was built, he had a job with four other guys building an airplane for a theatre, a mock up of an airplane. They were paid twenty-five hundred dollars. The five hundred dollars that my dad got paid wiped out the debt of buying this land and building this cottage. It was paid for in September 1938 by a 1939 Buick announcement meeting that they had to have an airplane for a Buick to come out of. There's a picture of that airplane here," he says pointing to a framed picture of an airplane with the Buick symbol on it. "So as a kid, you didn't know what a Depression was or that they even had a Depression."

"Five hundred dollars. That's amazing," I said looking around. "The camp itself isn't worth anything to anyone but us, but I wonder what the land is worth today."

"Over a quarter of a million dollars, as of a couple years ago. They'd tear down the house and build something bigger."

"We'll never let that happen, Gramp," I assure him. I know he worries about what will happen to Camp in the coming years when he and Gram aren't here any longer.

Quickly changing the subject, he says, "You should put in your notes that there wasn't a washing machine. Mother and Aunt Kitty cleaned the clothes out on the dock. The fireplace cost seventy-five dollars, twenty-five of which was the cast iron insert. The stonework was fifty bucks. That paid for the mortar and the helpers and the whole thing. But that was Depression time when money was something else."

Gramp worries that some day after he's gone, we are going to be in a position where we'll need to sell Camp. His concern is legitimate considering the economic state we are in here in America, but we will *never* let that happen. We remind him that each of us in the family is equally invested in maintaining Stagedoor and in keeping it in our family for many more generations. We will continue to work toward that common goal *together as a family.*

It is getting late and we are all tired. Gramp brings tonight's stories to a close by proudly declaring, "So at the end of the ten days, when it was time to get back to the theatre, Pop turned to look at his beautiful little summer cottage on the lake and decided to call it, appropriately so, Stagedoor."

CHAPTER 4
A Day on the Dock

~

I slip out of my Birkenstocks, leaving them on the sand at Robin's Trail behind me, as I step my bare feet, one at a time, onto the dock. The coldness of the aluminum under my feet sends a chill up my already cold body. I pull the sleeves of my oversized "Happy Camper" sweatshirt down over my hands and clench the extra material into my fists. I have just arrived at Camp for another summer vacation, and this is my annual check-in with myself. I think about where I am now compared to where I was at this time last year. I create new affirmations to replace any current, futile ones. Through this meditative pep-talk, I remind myself of who I am at the core…what makes me *me*…the things that keep me grounded…the things that I believe in…the things that I believe exist, in part, to inspire me. It is important that I never lose touch with any of that because if I do, that is when I become a stranger to my Self. I don't like losing touch.

Real people. Deep minds. Honest intentions. Class. Confidence. Confidantes. Eyes. Eye contact. Direction and drive. Not being perfect – being admirable. Soul relationships. Goals. Passionate people. Gentle kisses. People who live to love, laugh, and learn. Smiling. Traveling. Knowledge. Taking chances. Full body massages. People who challenge me. Love. The concept of love and the many forms it takes. Everyone I love. Making love. Falling in love interests me. Being in love motivates me. Staying in love inspires me. Mental and physical health. Connectedness. Oneness. Joshua Tree. Coloring. Dancing. Whispering. Vacillating. Skating. Laughing. Sharing secrets. Being rocked to sleep. Beethoven. The number 17. The one I spend the rest of my life with, and the one I spend the rest of my life loving. Missing the people I care about (it reminds me that we are real and fragile...alive and *here*). My park bench theory. Sweating. Being safe. Being naked. Asking questions. Taking pictures. Hard work. Parks with swings. Kelso Dunes. Being communicative. Human sexuality. Sensuality. Forgiveness. Letting go. A simple touch. Promises. Food. Not selling out. Paris and meeting You there. Being in the *moment. Open mindedness. Child rearing. Butterfly kisses. Heeding my intuition. Dreams and having someone with whom to share them.*

Being the best that I can be. Finishing what I start. Words. Diana Lynn. Genes. Reason. Being drug-free. Loyalty. Reflectors. Slow dancing. Loving deeply and not having to let go. Dying of old age. Not being afraid. Animals. Family. Friendship. Running. Hot wax from scented candles. American Sign Language. Wedding vows. <u>Little Women</u>. Being strong. My Puppy. Music from the 70's. Hugging. Giving birth. All five senses. Mylee. Self-actualization. The concepts of "wrinkles in the brain" and "luck." Reincarnation. Evolution. Playing games. Comfy clothes. Rose-scented anything. Seeing something beautiful in everything. Smiling from within. All four seasons. Human anatomy. Surprises. All of my parents, brother, Gram and Gramp and all that they represent. The view of the city from my tenth floor flat. Record albums. The Dewey Decimal System. Afternoon martinis outside London. Being true to myself. Controlled fire. Pillows and blankets. Fireplaces. Competition. When someone wipes a tear from your eye before you do. (That person loves you). What I smell the moment I turn onto the Dirt Road. Light knocks. Harmonicas and banjos. World Peace. Breath and balance.

I pause for a moment to take it all in before continuing to the end of the dock.

It is another cold, New England morning on the lake. The leaves on the trees behind me enjoy their morning stretch as the wind wakes them with a tender roar. A flock of ducks coasts by on the calm water before me. To the west, I see the sail of a boat waning in the distance. To the east, I see the gentle rise of the sun, marking the beginning of a new day.

I reach the end of the dock – my rock – standing as close to the edge as I can get without falling in. I curl my toes over the edge. I can still balance here, even with the breeze. I stand tall and straight, legs tight and ankles touching. I inhale as deeply as my lungs allow, tasting the crisp New Hampshire air. I raise my arms high over my head and clasp my hands together. I feel centered and strong. At last grounded, I am a warrior. In this moment, I have overcome.

Exhaling steadily, I sit down and prepare myself to come face-to-face with the lake once again. I roll up the bottoms of my gray sweatpants and toss my legs over the side. Pointing my toes like a gymnast (a warrior gymnast), they greet the water. Freezing.
Cold.
Warm.

I lean forward and look at the rippling circles my big toes make in the water. I inhale deeply once more, tuck my hair behind my ears, and close my eyes. The montage in my head begins.

Dad, Robin, Mark, and I have just arrived at Camp. Gram is in her garden and Gramp has just finished cutting the grass. We pulled up to find an enormous mound of sand that sat between us and the dock, blocking our view of the lake. Dad and Mark got right to their guy stuff building, fixing, and whatever it was they were always doing while Robin and I climbed to the top of this sandy mountain and proceeded to flatten it into a nice beach for the whole family to enjoy.

Dad and Robin met after our parents separated when Mark and I were five and three years old respectively. Robin and I have always been close, just as I have always been with Mom and Dad. She was a friend to me from the beginning. I do not remember life without her.

Robin never tried to take the place of Mom, so I was happy to make room for her. Naturally, the first few years after the separation were an adjustment for all of us. Sometimes, when Mark and I were with Dad and Robin, I missed Mom. Robin would let me cry. She was very good to me...always sensitive to what I was going through. I thought about this as the hill of sand beneath us became smaller and smaller.

Not long after that day, Robin was diagnosed with multiple sclerosis. She's been in a motorized wheelchair since. I have never once looked at her and thought, "She has multiple sclerosis." Instead, when I look at her I think, "She is my Other Mother."

I am twelve years old and I have just gotten my period. I woke up with it this morning. I had to tell Robin and I guess she told Dad. Someone had to. He knew something was wrong because I don't want to swim or ski today. Well, it isn't that I don't want to. I can't. What I don't want is my period. I will sit here on the dock until my arms and legs are covered in welts from my allergy to mosquitoes. I don't even care. I am angry and embarrassed, but my parents have always told me that when this day came, I should be excited and proud. They said it's my "initiation into womanhood." Why do they assume I want to be a woman? Who said I'm ready to stop being a kid? And why does that change in a moment's time? Without warning? There is no preparation for this time in a girl's life. Why doesn't Mark have to go through any of this? I hate being a girl!

Ahhhh, I sigh, smiling. I can still feel the upset from that day. As I remember, I did sit there until nearly sunset. Everyone in the cottage, Dad, Robin, Mark, Gram, and Gramp each strolled down at some point throughout that day. They came one at a time, bearing a bottle of water and something to eat. Each of them spoke to me, but I didn't think any of them understood what I was going through. I listened respectfully, but I didn't want to talk. I really just wanted to be left alone. After all, that was why I went to the dock in the first place.

I look to my right. The old wooden dock used to be over there. And I am two again. *I have just fallen off the dock, head first. Upside down and eyes wide open, I see a minnow swim by just as Dad picks me up by my left ankle and places me securely back on the dock.*
Cut to a panoramic view of the lake.

I glance over to the south end – the Sandy Beach. My brother is there. The water always felt warmer at Sandy Beach than it did out front of our camp, Stagedoor. *Sand...as far as we can swim. And no matter how far out we go, the water never rises above our chests.* Suddenly we are six and four again.

My gaze takes me to the center of the lake where Dad blew the engine of our 1976 California Ski Boat. It was the fastest boat on the lake. Everyone on the lake heard it – the loud, penetrating terror exploding from the engine. Everyone heard it. Well, everyone except me. They say I heard it, but that isn't how I remember it. I was out back in my own peaceful, nine-year old little world doing cartwheels and back handsprings off a mound of dirt that had been dug for some reason no one can remember today.

I can't even say that I *sort of* remember hearing it. I just know I was there.

Back at the Sandy Beach. It's 1987. The summer I learned to water ski. The first time I got up, I skied around the whole lake. I held on to the rope so tightly that my knuckles turned cold and white. I didn't know if I was any good, I just knew it was a lot of fun.

I've just come back to the dock after taking a bathroom break and changing out of my sweats and into my bathing suit. It's nearly 11 am. I fell asleep and thought I should get hold of some sun block. The sun is bright today and I don't want my skin to burn. It's a quiet day on the lake. Off in the distance, I can see the rooster tails of two jet skis and, about a hundred yards away, a slalom skier being pulled by a boat that resembles, to me, our old jet boat. I'm surprised there aren't more boats on the water today.

I lay my towel out to sit on. With the sun almost directly overhead, the aluminum would burn my skin. As I sit here today, applying Coppertone SPF 25, many thoughts race through my head with not enough time to process even one. I focus straight ahead on the bow of our 1963 Chris Craft Super Sport, the Music Mann, and I think:

I'm here alone with Gram and Gramp. God, how I love those two people. Will I ever marry or am I destined to be that lone gypsy child forever? Will I ever have children and will they have a relationship with this place? If I am to bear children, will they come soon, so they can know their great-grandparents?

All the years I've walked (or was carried, depending on my age at the time) on and off the different docks we've had. The night the wind swept my bathing suit right off the dock when my friend Deena and I were skinny-dipping. All the friends and family who have visited us here in the last seven decades since this place was built. Those I haven't met yet, but whom I will grow to love enough to wish to share this special place with. Roasting marshmallows on the beach with Tara and Steve. Floating over to Sammy Sands Campground with Robin, smuggling with us carrot and raison tuna sandwiches seasoned with curry. Creating the make-shift refrigerator by the dock with Jess so we didn't have to keep going back inside to get more drinks. Taking Gram on a sunset boat ride on her eighty-fifth birthday. Setting the minnow trap Mark and I would stick bread into to see how many minnows we could catch.

How we've all grown and how we'll all die. I can't believe our family's friend David has died. This place just isn't the same without him. Who will be next? If I think it's strange without David here, imagine how foreign it will be without Gram and Gramp.

Gram and Gramp are inside reading books and watching television. They sit next to each other on the couch. Sometimes, when neither of them is reading, I'll catch them holding hands. Gram, peering out from behind her reading glasses holds her bell-shaped lips in a delicate smile. She reaches up, without skipping a word on the page, to fix a strand of her soft gray hair that keeps tickling her forehead. Gramp, sitting so close to her that their slender legs are almost touching, watches politics on the television. He, through his eyeglasses, glances over at Gram every so often and smiles at her. When I see him do this, I can read his mind. He's saying, "Oh, how I still adore my bride." He whispers her name and waits for her to respond, reassuring him that she's really there. I've spent so many hours watching them that, even down here on the dock, I know exactly what's happening inside. Down here, it's just me and the dock - my rock. By now, the sun block has been (hopefully) evenly applied over my Irish/German and Russian/Hungarian skin. I shouldn't burn today.

I lie back relaxed and with a smile. I love the way the warm wind feels across my mouth and skin. I close my eyes again and listen to the tiny waves pour over the rocks on the shore behind me. Just then, my heart pounds with excited disbelief as I realize that I am actually *here* again – not just in my imagination. It always takes me a day or two of being here until I am assured that I'm not dreaming. Flipping over on my stomach, I prop my head up with my hands, and take panoramic snapshots with the lenses in my eyes. I'll save the digital shots for the rest of the year.

I focus on the pink milkweeds spiking out behind the rocks in this Granite State. The quartz is almost blinding as it sparkles in the sun. All different shapes, sizes, and colors. Some are darker because they're wet. Some are dry and darker just because they are. *Because they can be*, I remind myself. *Because they can be.*

A butterfly lands on the milkweed and stays there for quite a long time. I wonder: *What is the attention span of a Monarch butterfly?* Oh, what a beautiful picture that makes…with the bluest of skies above.

Blink.

And there I have captured it.

I turn my head to the north. I squint my eyes, as if there's really something there, and I see my nine year-old self on the dock practicing the dance I made up to *Dirty Dancing*'s "The Time of My Life."

Dirty Dancing was one of my favorite movies in the late eighties. Someone had given me the movie soundtrack and I danced around day after day pretending I was Baby practicing for my own performance. I remember thinking how grown up she seemed. I couldn't wait to be "a grown up" and to have boys want to dance with me. We rented the movie one rainy night that summer. That was the summer I wanted to be a dancer.

When the movie was over, Gramp looked at Gram and said with a smile, "That Jennifer sure has grown into a beautiful and talented young woman. Joel must be so proud of her."

Joel, I thought. *Who's that?* "Joel Grey – the guy on the wall over there?" I asked, pointing at the wall behind me, where Joel's picture hung between Liz and Rich's (whose full names I'd later learn were Elizabeth Taylor and Richard Burton) and Angie's (whose name, I'd later learn, was Angela Lansbury).

Beaches. That was my favorite movie in 1990 when Mom bought me the soundtrack. I'm not sure why it was my favorite movie because it was so sad, but I loved Bette Midler's voice and I knew every word to every song on the tape. I brought it with me to Camp that summer and listened to it until it began to warp. I was eleven years old. That was the summer I wanted to be a singer.

"Gramp, I wonder what Bette was like when she was my age."

"How about a teenager? Would you like to hear a story about her when she was a teenager?"

"Yes!" I exclaimed, "I can't *wait* to be a teenager!" I sat next to him on the couch trying not to blink. I didn't want to miss anything. I've always felt that way around Gram and Gramp. There is a lesson in everything they say and if they take the time to tell me something, I have always felt obliged – and honored - to hear it.

"The name of the show was 'Fiddler on the Roof.' Bette was probably about eighteen years old. There were three sisters and Bette was one of the sisters. You don't get paid very much when you have a small job in the theatre as an actress. Once a week I'd buy the *Time* magazine. I'd sit at my station and read it. Bette would keep her eye on me until I got to the last page, which might take until the next day, and then she'd come by and say, 'Hiya Jack! Are you through with your *Time* magazine?' and I'd say, 'Sure. Help yourself.' And away went the *Time* magazine; week, after week, after week. That was Bette Midler," he laughed reminiscently.

It's just after 2 pm, and the growling of my stomach has interrupted my thoughts. Just then, I hear Gram's loving voice call to me from the porch windows, "Lori, come on in, I've fixed us some lunch." Reaching the end of the dock, I step back into my shoes and make my way up Robin's Trail, listening as the soles of my shoes crush the tiny pebbles on the earth beneath them. Before heading inside, I stop for a moment to take in our little cottage. I have missed the wooden shingles that do such a stellar job at protecting our house during the brutal winter storms. I am grateful to them for keeping our special place safe for another year. Our Camp stands so small, yet so sturdy. Stocky – if a home can be stocky. *Thank you, Camp, for being so strong.* I use the brick slab walkway as I pass our picnic table and patio furniture and approach the front door. I stop to smell the daisies Gram has planted. I smile at the hanging plants and begin to open the door, stepping in a puddle on the ground where Gramp has just watered.

 Blink.

 And there I have captured it.

 With that, I go inside to enjoy lunch with two of my favorite people.

 It's 3:30 pm. I've just come back to the dock from a delicious lunch with Gram and Gramp. Turkey and cheese on toast with mayo, lettuce, tomatoes, pickles, and "no salt added" chips on the side with a large glass of 100% cranberry juice, diluted with water. *(Does that make it no longer 100% juice?)* Just a lovely lunch with two of my favorite, lovely people. We discussed their Camp projects for the afternoon. Gram has started a new painting and Gramp will fill the bird feeders, put air in the tires of my Chevy S10, and take the garbage to the dump.

 It sure is hot out here today. I jumped into the water a few minutes ago for a quick swim and to cool off. Now I'm back on the dock, reapplying some Coppertone to my face and shoulders, listening to an airplane overhead. I am reminded of the stunt man who used to fly his plane directly over our Camp. He did all kinds of circles and flips in that red airplane. I remember him from when I was just a little girl. He's retired now and we haven't seen his plane in a couple of years. Dad says he's dead. I guess that's a possibility. *Why wouldn't it be?*

Just as I am ready to lie back again, two teenagers ride past in a canoe. We smile and wave – say hello, and I can't help but notice the graceful ease with which they move. I watch them paddle, fascinated by their teamwork. And the montage continues.

I am nineteen years old and I am practicing yoga on the dock. I'm in my own little spiritual world this time, locked into feeling at one with nature and at peace with my place in the universe. Suddenly, I notice someone in a kayak, coming from Sammy Sands, a nearby campground, watching me. At first I am startled and embarrassed – I don't like being watched. Rather, I didn't realize I was being watched and I like to know things. As he glides closer, I wave and say hello. We strike up a conversation and I invite him to the dock. He stays for about ten minutes but then has to leave because his canoe is a rental and he has only fifteen minutes to return it. He invites me on a canoe ride with him tomorrow morning. I hesitate, so as

not to appear desperate for a summer friend, before saying
"Sure, we'll see."

It's nearly 7:00 pm when my nose captures the smell of hot dogs and hamburgers on the grills of nearby campers. *Mmmmm...Camp just wouldn't be Camp without that smell every night.* I was dreaming about the time when Mark was thirteen and took his boat, the Starcraft, across the lake to Western Lake Shores, another campground, for an evening dance with his "girlfriend" that summer. I wanted to go to the dance, but at eleven years old, Dad and Robin thought I was too young. They said I had to wait until I was "at least thirteen." *I wish I'd been adopted!* There actually was a time when I thought I'd been adopted for the plain and simple reason that Dad has hazel eyes, Mom's are brown, Mark's are blue (like Robin's) and mine are green. (When I later thought about a Presbyterian man and a Jewish woman producing an Atheist and a Skeptic, I momentarily examined that possibility again.) Anyway, Mark's curfew was 11:00 pm and I was determined to sit on the dock until he came back. *I'll show the family that I'm big enough to stay up that late.* Of course the mosquitoes got to me long before then and I was sound asleep on the porch by the time Mark got back.

I was pulled from my dream just in time to run inside and change out of my bathing suit and back into my sweats, before coming back to the dock to watch the sun set. I cannot believe this day has come and is nearly already gone. I mark an "X" through today's date on the calendar in my mind's eye. I know it's silly, but I feel disappointed for a moment because this sunset marks one less sunset I'll have at this Camp, on this dock, in this year.

It's 7:37. I sit on the center of the dock and face west. The trees grow dark, darker, until they appear black. I am awe-inspired by the electric reds, oranges, pinks, and purples that bleed across the sky, casting vibrant shadows along the mountain peaks. I wonder, *does Mt. Washington still, after all these years, appreciate the beauty that is shed upon it, night after night, year after year?* I watch Mt. Washington, so immense in all its glory, as it bathes in the magic of this evening's setting sun. It reflects true. *Does it, Mt. Washington, affect you?*

"Loooori…" I hear Gram's voice through the trees. She calls to me from the porch. "It's time for dinner."
I take another breath and smile as I stand up to begin my way back up the dock and out of the magnificence that envelops me. Rocks me. Soothes me. The magnificence that heals me.

Blink.

And there I have captured it.

CHAPTER 5
The Music Mann

~

Born to parents of the stage, it was no surprise that Gramp went on to work in the theatre as well. One might only assume that by growing up around so many famous and talented musicians, actors, and magicians, he would only follow. "I was almost born right at the stage door of the Palace Theatre," Gramp laughs. "My father took me to the funeral of a theatre when I was twelve years old. The Bijou Theatre in Battle Creek, Michigan. By that time it had been twenty-five percent dismantled and the walls were caving in. As in most old theatres, in the middle of the stage in the back was a very narrow stairway. So when my father told me I could go with him, he asked my mother if she'd like to go with us to the wake of the Bijou

Theatre. My mother said, 'I've been up and down those stairs enough times. I'll stay here and you guys go to the theatre.' So, Mother wouldn't come. I must have been bitten by something then.

As a kid, I spent twenty-four hours a day worrying about magic. And playing the clarinet at the same time. Magic and the clarinet. I had to walk from the schoolhouse down to the theatre to ride home with my dad at 3:30. They'd be rehearsing and they'd see this little kid walking in and they'd say, 'Oh, no! Get him off the stage!' I had my own seat right in the front and I wouldn't take my eyes off Harry Blackstone."

"Harry Blackstone is over there, right?" I point to a photograph on the wall near the kitchen. Gramp, not looking away from me, nods his head. He doesn't need to turn around. He knows where every photograph in this entire Camp is hung. "It's been there for seventy years."

"Harry Blackstone was a dear friend of my dad's. So I'd sit there every day and watch him rehearse. In the opening he produced stuff from nowhere and right toward the end he would steal his last load from underneath a pedestal. A girl was about to be exposed by the draperies coming apart. So you got six or eight girls up there but you can't see them. As you begin to see the first one, Harry Blackstone -- awkward as can be when you're watching him do it, but when it happens in the theatre you don't see him do it. He reaches here," Gramp gestures to his immediate left, "and gets the biggest load of stuff, including ducks and everything else -- he can hardly pick it up -- hooks it over his arm and walks downstage, just as this whole pretty picture opens up with the orchestra playing. And he proceeds to develop more stuff. So he's got a tub, a wooden tub -- low; he shows you it's empty by spinning it around and setting it down. All of a sudden water would come out of it as he slammed it back down again. And out of this empty tub would come three of the biggest ducks you have ever seen in your life! What did the ducks do? They walked across the stage into their little house that he had used previously for some piece of magic. So here's the duck house and they are trained to go right inside because there's food in there. So the three ducks walk in there like this..." he flattens out his hands, pretending they're a duck's feet.

"A guy comes across the stage and at a certain time the drummer blows a whistle. This guy runs across the stage, falls on his face, and slides offstage, like you have seen people do in the theatre. Guess what was happening while two thousand people were watching that guy slide offstage. There's a stagehand behind the scene with a rope tied to the duck house and the duck house is now offstage. But the duck house didn't move -- just the inside of it that had the three ducks. The duck house stayed there. So now Harry comes over and collapses the duck house and produces something else. The opening was like that –

ninety miles an hour! So I saw Harry Blackstone's act many, many times. He was the one who told me, 'Jack, there's not a single magician who it wouldn't be worth your while to go way out of your way to see perform, because he might teach you how not to do it.'"

Harry Blackstone was one of the great influences in Gramp's life as a child, who brought about his own talent in magic. When we were kids, Gramp would perform magic tricks for the four of us grandchildren. He was known for having mastered the skill of *sleight of hand*, a close-up type of magic typically involving cards or coins. Professional photographs from his performances hang on the same wall where Etta's showgirl picture hangs in Gram and Gramp's New Jersey home.

During his junior year of high school, Gramp formed a five-piece band called *Jack Mann and the Manhattans*, in which he played the clarinet. He played four nights a week through his last two years of high school at the Flushing Valley Country Club in Flushing, Michigan. In 1942, he began working in the theatre.

Gramp's first job was washing dishes at the Palace Theatre in Flint. "It was for a show called *Little Foxes* with Tallulah Bankhead. There was a little dining room on the set and I had to wash the dishes so they'd be clean for the next set. Many years later I did *Little Foxes* again with Elizabeth Taylor." In 1942, he also worked on the set of

The Man Who Came to Dinner, a three-act comedy show, and *Separate Tables*, a collection of one-act plays.

After he graduated from high school, he married his high school sweetheart, Jean Becker, originally from East Tawas, Michigan. They had met during their junior year when Gramp was campaigning for a friend of his who happened to be, unbeknownst to him, running against Gram for Junior Vice President of their class. Gramp approached the tall, thin beauty in hopes of gaining her vote.

"Did you vote for her, Gram?" I asked.

"Well, no I wasn't going to vote for her – I was running against her! Gramp didn't have a clue who I was. Anyhow," she said with the smile of a young teenager in love, "he asked me out on a date instead."

"Oh, I love it! Tell me about your first date!" By this time, Gram and I have switched seats. She and Gramp are sitting next to each other on the couch. I'm sitting still in the rocking chair, watching their every move.

"Do you want to tell her, Bud, or should I?" They smile at each other.

"Back then gas cost twenty-five cents a gallon. On that day, I picked her up for our luncheon date," Gramp begins.

"What did you guys order, do you remember?"

"I couldn't tell you what I had, but Mother here," he puts his hand on top of hers, which rests on her leg, "she ordered a sandwich. Too conservative to order a dinner. So on that date we had a sandwich." They look at each other again and smile. Gramp pats her leg.

"Gramp, didn't you tell her that night that you were going to marry her someday? Can you tell me that story?"

"You just said it."

"But I want to hear you say it." Gramp and I have a playful kind of relationship that I think is unique to the two of us. We have a distinct sense of humor, almost like we're teasing each other, and we're always making the other laugh. I smile while I wait for his response.

"You just told the story, Sis." It is late and he's getting tired. We've already been talking for several hours. I'd like to finish hearing this story tonight, but I am always sure never to rush them. I don't want the hurried version.

"I'll tell you the story, Lori," Gram says in her calm sing-songy voice, accenting the *ory* and *ori* just to be cute. I'm glad she's chiming in now. This will give Gramp a break from talking, and it will also prevent him from heading off to bed. He always wants to hear what Gram will say.

"You know how Gramp is with these mushy subjects," she begins.

"I do, which is why I wanted him to tell it," I throw a smile toward him with my eyes. He throws one back, shaking his head. He may be tired, but he still doesn't miss a trick. I just wanted that exchange with him to let him know that I don't either. We are a clever team, Gramp and me.

"Well, I remember, that was our first date," Gram begins. He took me home and we were sitting in his car. He looked at me and said, 'I'm going to marry you someday.' I was absolutely overwhelmed because up to that point no one had ever said anything like that to me. Nobody in my family had ever said 'I love you'. I never heard it until then. I really don't remember what I said to him or if I said anything at all, but I would assume we probably hugged and kissed after that. I just don't remember. That was a long time ago," she giggles.

"What kinds of things did you do on dates?"

"Oh, well, we always went to either the Palace to see a movie or to the I.M.A. Auditorium to dance and see a band play. We loved to dance! And both places were free for us to go to anytime we wanted because they were all friends with Gramp's father."

They were married that fall, on October 8, 1942. Three months later, Gramp left for his four-year stint in the military, where he played clarinet in the 681st Army Air Force Band. He spent the first two years in Indianapolis, traveling to places such as Syracuse and Rome, New York, and Riverside, California. Then he began his trek to China aboard the USS Mann. Thirty-two days after leaving the

United States, he, along with five thousand guys and five hundred marines arrived in Bombay. It took them over a week to get from Bombay to Calcutta where they continued on to Burma and eventually China.

Gramp got out of the military on May 15, 1946, and returned to Michigan, where he reunited with his bride. That summer, Gram made her first visit to Stagedoor. Eleven months later, in July 1947, she gave birth to their first child, Mary Katherine Mann, my Aunt Kay. Gramp spent the next five years working in maintenance in the theatre, doing jobs such as changing light bulbs, putting coal in the hopper, and changing the attraction board. "It was an apprenticeship," he explained. "There are mechanical things that you need to learn about the theatre, but to feed your family you have to do maintenance while you're there."

In 1951, G. Smiley Robertson, electrician at the I.M.A Auditorium died. When he died, Gramp took his job. Two years later in April 1953, their second child, Brian Edward Mann, my father, was born. Gramp continued working in the theatre, but it would still be another eight years before he'd make his mark in Broadway history.

Being so modest, and now weary, I wasn't sure how Gramp would respond to the rest of my questions tonight. He knows how important it is to me to capture these stories for the generations to come, though. As we continued our chat that evening, I looked at him with a sincere impression of pleading in my eyes. "How did it all begin, Gramp? How did you get to New York?" I asked. I was about to learn that the story was quite a simple one. I found it fascinating, nonetheless, probably because I find everything about Gram and Gramp to be fascinating.

"I worked in the theatre in Michigan for thirteen years," he began. "I'd gone to New York with the ambition of becoming a lighting director. A friend of mine from Flint, Robert Maybaum, who had only been in New York for three weeks, was operating the sound on a musical called *Do Re Mi*. I arrived the night of the show, and I knew some of the guys in the crew who took me to the opening night party. And the scuttlebutt was saying this was the last show that Al Alloy was gonna light. The designers decided that if a designer couldn't light his own show, he had to go out and hire one of their brothers to do it. So, Al Alloy decided that was his last show. That night, though, I saw the stage ablaze with light! Never have I seen a stage lit up that way. Anyway, so I found out why that scuttlebutt was going on. That was the end of my idea of being a lighting director. As a scene designer I wasn't interested. The date was December 26, 1959.

So, now my mother's up in Boston living with her sister. I go up there to spend a few days with them and get something to eat since I'm not gonna be a lighting director. While I was there, the Boston Globe came out with a two-column review of a show. One-third of the review was about how bad the sound was. It had previewed in Boston the night before. '*Show Girl,* with Carol Channing, opened to bad reviews,'" he said as if quoting the review. The bad reviews were mostly due to problems with the sound. Mother said, 'For Pete's sake, Jack, why don't you go down there and fix it for them? It would be a shame for them to have to close the show.' Little did she know, being a showgirl, that that's not the way you get a job in sound.

So I got back from Boston to my apartment in New York, which would be the 3rd of January, and I stopped by an electrical shop owned and operated by Meyer Harris. He had this little shop at 47th and 8th Avenue and I knew him quite well. And I didn't notice, I'm in the back having coffee, and Meyer made a phone call. And I found out in a few minutes that the phone call was to Masque Sound getting an interview for me from Masque the next day.

The next day I go to Masque Sound to meet Sam Saltzman, one of the owners. Big long interview speech. Terrific fellow. And he says, 'Well, you go back to your apartment, sit by your telephone and the worst that will happen, we'll find you a job.'

The next day at one o'clock, he called and said, 'Meet me at the Eugene O'Neill Theatre.' He already had a job for me in less than twenty-four hours. The secret was that Meyer Harris gave him the secret word *Potash and Perlmutter.* So he says 'When you go to get this job, don't say a word to the manager except *Potash and Perlmutter.*

So I do, and the general manager looks at me over his Cyclops glasses, his overcoat was this far off the ground, typical Broadway show general manager, 'How long have you known Meyer Harris?' I said, 'Fifteen years.' So on and so on and, I got the job. I rushed back to the shop the next day after doing the show that night and I said, 'What does *Potash and Perlmutter* mean?' He says, 'Jack, in 1920 and '21, Mike Goldryer, your manager, and I had a burlesque act in Lower Manhattan, at which time we had the opportunity to help an awful lot of people. Those two old guys spent their lives helping people…because if you haven't heard it yet, you have very little to do with your next job. Your next job comes from somebody you don't even know, which is the case in me. For the next ten, twelve years, every job I got was because of Jonathan Tunick. I had no idea! So there I go, gettin' the job that Mother had set out for me to get in the first place."

"What was the problem with the sound on the Carol Channing show, Gramp?"

"HA!" he laughs. "The sound system was backwards on the stage. It was up against the wall and all the knobs were against the wall - the cement wall - of the theatre. And the knobs were all taped to the certain position when it came from Boston. So Sam says, 'Meet me at the theatre at 3:30.' I had from 3:30 until show time to fix the sound."

"What did you do first?"

"First we moved it and put it up in the box where it belongs – or at least where I thought it belonged. But they didn't have sound systems up in the box. 'Who's this guy putting sound systems up in the box?' they thought. Unheard of! They had them underneath things, in the basement, crazy places, never where the operator had a fighting chance. Carol Channing was a favorite of mine. Her husband sat beside me for the whole twenty-two weeks. Never said a word. He just sat there. He heard everything she said, and he was a happy man."

During *Show Girl*, Gramp ran into someone who needed his help on George Abbott's show, *Beckett*. The person in charge of designing the sound for that show had taken a week off and the person they put in charge of the sound was not a "soundy." Gramp, always eager to help someone out, offered to run the first three or four cues for him before each show since *Show Girl* opened thirty minutes after *Beckett*. That is when Gramp became acquainted with Mr. Abbott, and he did every one of his shows from then until Mr. Abbott died.

"Gramp, you have been called the man who 'revolutionized sound' and 'one of the great pioneers of sound design.' I'd love to hear a story about something you did that no one had done previously." Again, I was apprehensive as to how he would respond, but I didn't feel like rejection was in the air that night. I can't write a book based on my assumptions, so if he chose not to respond, we'd be at a stalemate. *I know this book is just as important to Gramp as it is to me.*

There is a fine line between sharing the details of one's past and bragging about them. Gramp would never want to be mistaken for the latter. That is why his words are always calculated. After a moment, he looked at me and began, "I sleep out on the porch up here in the summertime and facing me is a mile and a half of water by six miles of water. Every night at nine-thirty a train comes to town, a steam engine in those days, 1951, maybe. I'm trying to figure out. How come those engines sound so loud when they get even with us? They were right in my bed! That's how loud these things were. So I have to figure out why. It's pretty simple, but it took me a long time.

I went back to the theatre in Michigan and built a series of doghouses and put the microphones in the doghouses instead of on the stands. That was an improvement but the management wouldn't stand for it. It looked a little ridiculous. So then I turned the RCA 77s - big, big microphones - on their side, put a little sponge underneath, tried four of those and see what I had. And that was a step in the right direction. Then I found little pencil microphones. There was only one of them where the head was made of gold. AKG 451 had a metal diaphragm which was made by a man in a little laboratory from gold. You can buy any kind you want of them, but this is the microphone that works. So I got one on the floor and it worked alright. Carol Channing had them on the floor; all those little Japanese men [*Pacific Overtures*] had them on the floor. I had a lot of calls where I had to put them on a shaggy carpet. Now, acoustically, how's a fellow gonna do a sound job if the carpet is shaggy carpet? Not just regular carpet, but shaggy rug carpet! HA! Well it's easy. You take an AKG microphone, they built a swivel for me a long time ago, you cut a hole in the carpet, you put the body of the mic covered, the head of the mic uncovered, and turn it down forty-five degrees. (The name of the show was *Love for Love*.) I'll never think of the lady's name but she had one of them in the center of her set and she wandered around. Sounded like a million dollars. One microphone. You don't have to do it that way but you won't get Jack Mann Sound if you don't. And the little lady will come and say, 'That doesn't sound like Jack Mann to me!'"

"Gramp, I know you didn't get credit for many of the shows you did in the beginning of your career, but you received credit in another form when you did a show with Liz. Which show was that?" *I know this story; I've heard it many times. It's one of my favorites because the happiness in Gramp's voice when he tells it has remained consistent since the first time I heard it.*

Gramp smiled and crossed his legs. "Every once in a while, something happens that turns you around and you can see where you really are. You may have got a little whiff of that previously, but this will hit you harder.

Hopefully. The show was called *Private Lives* - Elizabeth Taylor and Richard Burton. It has a moving stage so you can bring the whole thing down front on twelve big castors. She decides to troupe it for many weeks, so Gram and I had a nice job for a bit, staying in nice hotels. One of the arrangements was the Copely Plaza in Boston. Elizabeth comes in, sees the manager, and he offers to give her a suite without charge and she says, 'Providing you'll give the crew the same financial exchange.' So the whole crew for *Private Lives* is living in the Copely Plaza for cheap. Beautiful place. That's Elizabeth. So the show is about to close, and it happens to be my birthday. There are certain things that happen at the end of a show. Liz had bad legs, so somebody had to help her down from the step and I was elected early on. So every night I helped Elizabeth get down this step that was higher than an average step, and tonight she doesn't disappear. Richard appears over here, some more of the cast over there, some more of the crew over here. All of a sudden a guy comes out with a cake and they sing happy birthday to Jack. If you can imagine! Elizabeth's singing up a storm and her legs are killing her. She wants to get back into the dressing room. People are really something. So it all adds up to a gold watch on Christmas."

Getting back to sound, Gramp continues, "People like Mr. Abbott and Hal, they wanted it out of sight – a secret. They also wanted it so you couldn't hear it. They didn't know that at the time, but we had to educate these people or we'd starve to death. But if you fought them, you wouldn't eat any better. So I always put stuff behind the drapes. I did that for years. There's nothing more exciting than making sound work because the hum and distortion is terrible if you're aware of it."

"How come you didn't get credit for so many shows?" I asked somewhat defensively. Mark had recently searched for "Jack Mann Broadway" on the computer and found the Internet Broadway Database (IBDB)[1] which allowed him to then navigate to a page including a list of many of the shows Gramp has done. Upon seeing the list himself, Gramp informed us of the many inaccuracies it contained. In it, he is listed as a designer and a performer, though he was never a performer. Additionally, the IBDB has him listed as only having designed sound for thirty-three shows, when he claims to have worked more than that.

Show Girl was the first of more than forty shows in twenty-six years for which Gramp designed sound for the Broadway stage. It was the work he did on this show that made him the first person in theatre history to earn the official title of Sound Designer.

---

[1] Gramp and I have both contacted IBDB on several occasions in attempt to rectify this discrepancy. Unfortunately, none of our attempts were ever acknowledged.

"I am *so proud* of you, Gramp," I told him that night. He's had the privilege of working with such renowned people as George Abbott, Leonard Bernstein, Harold Prince, and Stephen Sondheim. I look around at the photograph-covered walls of Camp. There are Playbills from some of the shows Gramp did. *Milk and Honey, Fiddler on the Roof, Company, Follies, A Little Night Music, Gypsy, Pacific Overtures, Sweeney Todd, West Side Story, Baby, The Tap Dance Kid, Oliver!...*

Though Gramp enjoys talking about his work, he has remained most humble. He is modest when others, in his case, might not be. Every time we talk about his job, I find it harder to comprehend how I made it to my late teens before realizing just who my Gramp is.

I dabbled in acting during my freshman year in high school. I spent many nights in the theatre after school until ten o'clock or later, but I wasn't any good, so my interest in acting was fairly short-lived. However, it was during that year when I found out that "Hal" was "Harold Prince" – producer and director of some of the best-known musicals in Broadway history.

Later that year, I was rehearsing a monologue for an audition for the spring musical. I can't remember the show it was from, but at the bottom of the page, I read "Written and Directed by Stephen Sondheim." I shook my head in surprise, and then shook it again after deciding I shouldn't be surprised. *Of course "Steve" would be Stephen Sondheim. Why wouldn't it be?*

"Have I not been paying attention, or what, Gram?" I asked a little frustrated but still beaming with pride, motioning with my entire arm toward Gramp. "Why didn't anyone ever tell me this?"

"Well, I don't know, Lori," Gram giggles. "It was our job. It was what we did."

"What exactly did you do in the theatre, Gram?" Gram leans back in her rocking chair and begins the story of her work in the theatre. As I sit across from her, Indian-style on the couch, I study her closely, and I wonder how I could claim to know her so well when I was hearing this for the first time.

"Well, Gramp had a company called Theatre Sound. It was a group which involved sound, lighting, and building the scenery." This is the first I had ever heard of Gramp having a company. I shake my head again. "I took care of the office for Theatre Sound, Gram continues. "I did the bookkeeping and everything for the office. I didn't get paid for anything but I was in the Program as his assistant. At that time he was called the Electrician and I was the Assistant to the Electrician. When he was eventually in the Program as Sound Designer, I was [his] Assistant. I drove into the Bronx everyday from Hillsdale, that's when I first started working with him. I was always back at home before your dad got home from school. I did that until he graduated and then I started working in the theatre with Gramp. I knew all these people, so it was only natural that I would work with them.

I went all over the theatre and checked sound levels. I checked to see whether they were in phase. I helped him actually tune the theatre. We did that everywhere we went with each show. During the performance, I was in the audience and I took notes on the different people in the show…whether you could hear them right or if there was anything wrong. Then we'd go back to the theatre and discuss it for two or three hours every night after the show until seven or eight o'clock. We did that until the show opened. Sometimes I sat with the director and the lighting guy and whoever else had to be there. Sometimes they would tell me something that had to be done or what they didn't like and I would relay that message back to Gramp.

All of that was while we were "in production" meaning out of town, you know, before they brought the shows into New York. We went all over. You know we were in London, but I did the same thing everywhere we went. Then even after opening night in New York, I would still sit in the audience and take notes or stand back in Sounding Room. I sometimes would stand back there and listen and take notes. That's where Angela [Lansbury]'s husband would always stand because he was always concerned about her. This was when she was in *Sweeney*

Todd. That kind of thing. I could go back to Gramp and say it wasn't too good on Angela. I knew how to listen because I knew what "phase" meant. We primarily worked with phase because that's what makes people sound good. I would report back to him so he could make adjustments and that's what we did.

I usually sat in Hal Prince's seat. He had me sit there to check the levels and to be sure that everyone could be heard. I did that for several years. It was a good time in my life. A very good time in my life. I enjoyed it. I loved being with all of those people. It was nice to know that I was contributing, you know? They were all very nice to me. They were all such great people."

"How come you never told me any of this?" I looked at them, baffled. Gramp's response to my question was simple and, in that respect, much like Gram's. "My father found that all the people he worked with were beautiful people and I found that not a single one of the people I worked with wasn't just a first class, working person. They weren't actors. They were people who happened to have a job acting and they were wonderful people. I had a good relationship with all of them. That's the whole story and Mother and I would never think it was 'interesting' or anything else. Their job was to act; my job was to design the sound; your job is to work and keep going to the schoolhouse. It's a job. That's all it is, Sis."

And that was it, just like that. That's all he said. I, quite possibly not as modest as those in my family, could have lived a far less miserable life during middle school had I known this information. In that moment, I was certain that, as the new girl in seventh grade, being the granddaughter of such a respected sound man on Broadway would have been an immediate "in" with the theatre kids.

"I was on vacation for forty-five years, Sis." With that, he retreated to bed.

CHAPTER 6
Like You

~

I cleaned up from dinner tonight. (It was Gram's turn to cook.) I decided that I am too tired to stay awake for our nightly chat. I feel drained from being in the sun all day, so after my shower, I kiss Gram and Gramp goodnight and retire to the porch. Once there, however, I am unable to rest. I think about Gram and Gramp in the living room – eight feet away from where I lie, watching a Turner Classic movie. I think about their ages. On their next birthdays, they are going to turn eighty-six and eighty-seven years old. I wonder how many more years they are going to be coming up to Camp by themselves...living here by themselves from May to October, when none of us are here. They're beginning to have a hard time getting around up here. I look around the porch, but the darkness prevents me from seeing much. Instead, my gaze leads me through the windows to the moon, which gently bounces across the lake.

Being at Camp is a time when I completely relax. I am never happier than when I am here. My thoughts drift away from the "clock-punching" fast-paced society from which I've come and toward the slower, "stop and smell the roses" mentality of a New-Englander. Tucked in beneath a sea of blankets, I meditate to the sound of the water caressing the rocks outside. I close my eyes and take deep breaths as the cool, summer breeze drifts in through the windows and washes over my face. I am one with these woods.

After a few minutes, my thoughts go back to Gram and Gramp. While Gramp and I spend a lot of time talking up here, Gram and I spend a lot of time doing things, in addition to talking. We enjoy driving to the clothing outlets in town, stopping for lobster rolls at the Sandspring Restaurant, and doing creative projects together, like painting, tie-dying clothes, and making candles. We're busy going places and doing things, but we're even busier talking. There is rarely a moment of silence between Gram and me. I struggle to describe my relationship with her in words because what we share is a feeling. The connection we have is different from that of Gramp and me, but it is every bit as intense.

I'm too tired to talk tonight, but my mind needs to release this traffic…to write unedited. Unplanned. Unchanged…the stream of consciousness that is my only savior in times like these. I reach for a pen, place it on a page in my journal, and by the light of the moon, I write.

Dearest Gram,

You are the wisest woman I know, perhaps because you're the oldest, or perhaps because you're just wise. Everything I want to say is just a short distance from the pen my hand holds – a short distance to my heart where I can feel everything I want to share with you.

I have always justified your wisdom by the number of years you've spent in your skin, by the number of miles your bones have carried you. It is ironic that the number of years I've spent roaming this Earth seems directly correlated to the amount of confusion I have come to experience as an adult. The older I become, the less I understand of the things I thought I once knew.

I learn from you all the time. Just this morning you worked with me through my innately pessimistic beliefs on unconditional love. We sat on the porch sipping tea. I told you that I did not believe people were capable of such love in romantic relationships. I believe that we, as humans, feel and think and act based on conditions. We have minds with feelings that get hurt, that doubt, that mistrust. We are, indeed, products of our environment, and so we enter into relationships based on these conditions.

You asked me if I believe it exists at all, among any creatures. I said that perhaps the only kind of unconditional love, is a parents love for their child, or a cockers love for his owner. I lower my eyes, missing Springer, my cocker spaniel that died a couple of years ago.

When Mom was carrying me in her womb, she sometimes sat in her rocking chair. She would hold her growing belly and wonder how I would turn out, what I would look like, and if I would grow up to love her as much as she already loved me. From the time I was born, she would rock me to sleep in that chair. As a toddler, she would hold me on her chest, facing her. My tiny legs would fit through the wooden pegs that supported her back. I would lay my head on her chest. I could hear her heart beat through my left ear and, through my right ear, I could hear the music from the record player. I am lucky to have experienced that type of love from Mom, Dad, and Robin, but I do not believe anyone else is capable of expressing that pure level of love and having it be received with the same level of purity. Love that is not pure cannot possibly be unconditional.

I wish I could be more like you, Gram. I guess I'm just not, though. I could never be like you.

You disagree with me completely. Whole-heartedly. Absolutely. In fact, I can still hear the disappointment in your voice... a solemn disappointment in me for even thinking that way. It has echoed in my mind all day. I looked at you sitting before me. I watched you as your arms rested on your legs and you made perfect figure eights with your thumb and forefinger. You told me that your mother always did that. I wonder if she knew when she did it. I wonder if you

Know when you do it. Do you? Your slightly damp, sad eyes looked into mine, just as damp and sad, as if to say, "Dear, sweet Grandchild, if you learn nothing else from me, learn this."

Everything about you is beautiful, starting with your name. Jean E. Becker, "Jo" Mann. You were born on a farm in East Tawas, Michigan, in 1922. Nineteen *twenty-two*. You are one of your mother's five children to survive the first few months of life, and you're the only one who was born in a hospital. Though you lived in a tent with a dirt floor through part of the Depression, you have told me, "It was really not difficult." You are the strongest person I know. You have survived so much.

For many years on Christmas, your mother knitted you and all four of your brothers a cap or a scarf and a pair of mittens from sweaters people had given her that year. Those two articles of clothing, along with an orange, were your Christmas gifts. As an adult, you said you still can't imagine where she would have gotten those oranges. I loved when you recalled that "They were those really big, beautiful ones that cost a dollar-something now." You understand the true meaning of recycle.

You and your brothers are all still alive today; your birth years range from 1916 to 1937. Each of you has made it through your own suffering — suffering that I have never known: burying your parents and all of your friends, poverty, and war.

You've told me that your earliest memory is one that you can see as clearly today as if it just happened. You were three years old. Every day, you watched your mother dress your newborn baby sister, Myrtle. You were always eager to hold her, but Myrtle was very ill. She had been born with spina bifida. One morning, you watched your mother dress her and begged to hold her. You couldn't understand why she kept shooing you away. You later learned the reason was because your sister had died in the night and your mother was dressing her for the funeral.

You grew up without a telephone, a television, and a radio, sometimes even without electricity. For fun, you told me that you and the kids in the area would play games, read books, or make fudge.

You say you were always reading a book. You loved the Big Little Books. Still today you do not go a whole day without reading. You'll read just about anything you can find, from "Chick Lit" to Nicholas Sparks to James Michener and Jodi Picoult. That is why your mind is still so sharp. I'm glad I've gotten you more interested in memoir lately. I love when we read the same books and talk about them. You should have been awarded an honorary Master of Arts degree in Writing when I graduated because you read almost everything I did. I feel like we graduated together. That is one more experience that keeps us close.

You've told me that you always loved to read because it allows you to escape from your life and delve into the lives of the characters. You especially enjoyed reading during the time you spent living in the tent because the stories allowed you to go back to some of the places you once knew, cracking hazelnuts with all your might and adding some to the homemade fudge, picking daisies and twirling in the fields. It's all very

"Anne of *Green Gables*." You treasured those stories because, during that time, you didn't know when you'd ever see a hazelnut again, among other things. You read your books and just pretended. They helped you feel comfortable. Safe.

You are an artist. Your favorite flower is a daisy and to find many of your watercolor paintings without at least one is impossible. You love to garden, just as your mother always did. Now, when you garden, you say you can feel your mother's presence.

Daisies everywhere - white, yellow, cosmos, beautiful shades of pink and white. I love to watch you in your garden. Every so often, you lift your hand to brush the fine grey hair away from your eyes. You delicately place the stray hairs back to where they belong and continue on with your work.

Your hands are soft and gentle as you finger the petals with the tender touch of nearly ninety year-old hands. You wander gracefully from flower to flower. Your body, long and thin, still stands five feet, seven inches tall. When you concentrate, you close your red, bell-shaped lips — the top resting delicately but deliberately on the bottom. Even when you're asleep, they are shaped like a smile. You are without a doubt a happy woman.

I am without a doubt lucky.
You are my Gram. Always a lady. Optimistic to a fault.
You know how it is to suffer.
You have lived.
You understand what it means to overcome.
You are a hero in my life.
It would be impossible for you to let me down.
You overflow with all things great.
You are sweet and giving, patient and selfless.
Yes, you are a lady.
You are prim and proper and sincere.
You are a genuine lover of life.
You wake every morning with happy anticipation of a good day ahead, and always with a smile on your face.
You are an enthusiastic wonder.

You have always eaten all the right foods and you still follow the same daily exercise regimen you started when you were eighteen years old. A cigarette has never touched your lips. I have never heard you utter a curse word. You have been in love just once. You are living proof that wholesome exists.

You've advised me that the first thirty years of marriage are the hardest, and "if you can get through that, you can get through anything." When I asked, you told me that your most prized possession is your family. Then, like Gramp, you added, "If you can call that a possession." You consider the most profound event in your life to have been when Dad and Aunt Kay were born, "...seeing them for the first time."

I have this tremendous fear that one day, after you and Gramp leave this life, there will be one specific question that I never thought to ask you...a question that no one else knows the answer to. And I will never know because wherever you go, it will be to a place where I can't reach you. That's why I always ask you both haphazard questions. Then we wind up talking for hours and wonder how we got started on the subject in the first place. You are my best friend. I love you to the depths.

The other morning at breakfast, I asked you to tell me what the happiest and saddest days of your life were. You responded immediately, as if you'd been waiting for me to ask that specifically. The happiest day of your life was your wedding day and the saddest day was when your mother died.

I cannot imagine my wedding day, or the day either of my mothers dies. I sat there, paralyzed, waiting for you to say something more.

"But it was a blessing, too, when my mother died. A bittersweet blessing." I'm not sure I'll be as positive when it's my turn. I could never be like you.

You value your patience above all, and you have said with a surefire smile that if you could go back and start all over again, you wouldn't change a thing. I looked at you in sheer amazement. If given the opportunity, Gram, I would change things.

You believe strongly in family and self-worth and caring, in caring about yourself, and in making sure you're the kind of person people will be happy to be with and want to be like. It is important for everyone to have someone they admire in their lives, especially the kids. But you are a role model to us all. Thank you for that.

When it comes to love, you talk about "The Five C's." I lie back on the bed and try to remember all five. After a moment, I can recall them: Communication, commitment, compassion, consideration, and compromise.

According to you, "The Five C's" is the key to every successful relationship. "If you haven't got plenty of all five of those, you haven't got a relationship," you say. I wonder how anything can be that simple, but I want to believe that it can be.

You once told me that I am one of your precious treasures. That is precisely how I feel about you. When we drive together, you are my precious cargo. You are a gem, an honest soul, a living angel.

You impress upon me your words of wisdom. You share with me your secrets, and how you came by them. You are generous with your advice. You speak from experience, with knowledge. And when you speak, I listen.

Oh, but Gram, could I ever be like you?

I, too, was born in a hospital, but I went right to a two-story home -- one with three bedrooms and a big backyard. I wasn't permitted to play in the dirt, let alone to sleep on it. I have nine scarves, twenty-three hats, eight pairs of gloves, and I eat an orange every day. I have seen disease and I have seen death, but I have never buried a sibling or a parent. I grew up with a telephone, a television, and a radio. I never slept in the dark because I was afraid of it. I, too, would play games and read books, but I never knew there were hazelnut trees and I certainly didn't know how hard they were to crack. I did, however, and still do, love _Anne of Green Gables._

"Recycle," to me, means "put the newspapers in this bin and the cans and bottles in the other." My writing is my art. My journal is my garden. One day, when you leave me to rejoin your mother in hers, your presence will remain about me when I write, as your mother's has remained about you when you garden. I will still miss you with every fiber of my being. I cannot imagine the extent to which I will miss you.

I could never be like you because I am like me — unique and plenty good enough.

I may not be as graceful as you are, but as I lie here tonight, concentrating, I can't help but notice the same delicate but deliberate placement of my lips.

I understand suffering in my own way and perhaps I am a hero to someone else. What I lack in character, I make up for in spirit. I'm far from as wholesome, but I'm just as sincere. The best and the worst days of my life have yet to come, but I continue to learn from you. When you talk, I listen.

If you can look back on your life and honestly tell me that you wouldn't change a thing — even with all the bad — I can certainly look forward to my wedding day, my children's wedding day, and all the "bittersweet blessings" in between with the same mindset. And I shall embrace each of those moments. Each of those unknowns.

Thank you, Gram, for all that you've done. Thank you for receiving my words as I have always received yours. And thank you for loving me (unconditionally) and for believing in me especially in times I didn't quite believe in myself. I love you.

Always,
Lori Jill

CHAPTER 7

The Show Must Go On

~

One gloomy afternoon at Camp, while I was in the shed switching over my laundry, I stumbled across my friend David. I stumbled across David's remains, actually. Cancer had gotten him a year and a half earlier and all that was left of him was right there in a small white cardboard box on the floor in the shed tucked away under the cabinet. The box that housed his remains read in black typed font:

White Mountain Crematory

David R.S. Gingham

0703698

One glance at that number, and I had it memorized. One look at that tiny box. *Our friend David has been reduced to a seven-digit number on a tiny white box.* Whoever would have thought that his six-foot two-inch frame could fit inside such a small box?

David didn't have any family. Rather, our family was his family. His girlfriend, Ann Marie, organized a memorial service for him up at the lake early last summer, but I couldn't make the trip from New Jersey to his home in New Hampshire because of work obligations. Ann Marie, the thoughtful woman she is, decided to save some of his remains for me to spread once I made it back to Camp in August. She knew what kind of loss David's death was for me, as she recognized the trueness of our relationship. For some reason, though, and I don't know why, we never spread the rest of his ashes once we were all up there that summer. I don't believe I knew, at the time, that some of his ashes had been saved for me. If I did, I do not remember. It wasn't until this summer, in 2008, when what was left of David was returned to the earth, from which it came fifty-two years prior.

He was my dad's best friend. They were babies together and they spent their summers playing and exploring on the lake at Camp. They were neighbors. Their fathers grew up together. David never had any kids for Mark and I to grow up with, so we grew up with him. We all loved David dearly. He was a second son to Gram and

Gramp, and when they started growing older, David took it upon himself to stop by Stagedoor everyday to check on them. He was a fantastic chef and he always brought with him his most recent creations. They would talk about "old times" when he and my dad were young boys. I loved listening to their stories. Before I knew it, David and I had stories of our own. We grew especially close during the last five years of his life when I spent a month up at Camp every summer. We'd go boating and/or skiing every day, and if it rained, we'd talk on the phone.

Mark and Staci came up to Camp for a couple of days this month. Dad and Robin were here with Gram, Gramp, and I for the whole week. One afternoon while everyone was down by the dock drinking beer and relaxing in the water, I sat at the picnic table out back and wrote. At around two o'clock that afternoon, I saw Mark walking up Robin's Trail toward the table where I was sitting.

"Little Sister, what'cha doin'?"

He'd come up to the Camp to get a couple more beers and bring them back to the dock. I told him that I was contemplating taking a walk down Haverhill Trail to David's house.

"Why would you do that?" he asked.

"Because. Cuz I miss him." I felt my eyes fill with tears.

David was fun and funny and part of me doubted that he was dead. I *knew* he was dead, but somewhere in the folds of my soul, I didn't quite believe it. I couldn't feel it. But I missed him terribly. He died in that house and I thought that being there could help me to feel close to him again. To miss him less. To heal more. To remember. He was my summertime best friend and I just missed him.

"I want to hop the fence into his backyard and climb into his house through a window." I began telling him my plan. David had been dead for seventeen months, but there wasn't a doubt in my mind that his windows weren't locked. They hadn't even been boarded up. No one had even been in there to go through his things after he died. I imagined crumbs from his toast still on the seat of his recliner – the remote on the left armrest; his clothes still in the basket waiting to be folded; his toothbrush still on the bathroom sink. I imagined the sweet scent of his cigars still lingering in the air and food still in his refrigerator. I imagined the reality was not that he was dead, but that he just wasn't home.

Just then, Dad came up the Trail. He saw that I was upset and asked what was wrong. I looked down and shook my head as if to say, "Nothing. Everything's OK," knowing that he'd know then that I just didn't want to talk about it. He looked at Mark and repeated his question. Mark glanced at me as if saying, "I don't want to 'tell on' you, but going to David's isn't a good idea and maybe the two of us can talk you out of going there." The only reason why I didn't want Dad to know, aside from that I knew he wouldn't approve (though I wasn't concerned about that at the time) was because I knew it would upset him. After all, David was his lifetime closest friend.

Mark asked me not to go and Dad said I'd be completely stupid if I did. He said if anyone saw me on his property and called the police I could be charged with trespassing. He added that if someone saw me going into his house, I could be charged with breaking and entering. I added that I would just tell the cops to fuck off and that the town they work for should have done something with the house in the first place. I was angry that, seventeen months later, his property was still untouched. It made me sick to my stomach that all of his belongings still sat inside that house as though he'd placed them there that morning. It was like no one cared. No one but us. We cared. And we were all so sad.

I decided to wait until after Mark, Staci, Dad, and Robin left to go back to New Jersey before I went to David's. Then they wouldn't have to know...until I told them. I thought about waiting for Deena to come up and asking her to go with me. Or Jess. She'd be up shortly after Deena left and she could be my lookout. I wondered which one of my two friends I could put up to a possible brush with the law. I ultimately decided on Jess.

I was afraid when I imagined sneaking over to my friend's house, yes. Perhaps I was a little foolish to want to put myself through that, emotionally, but I needed to smell him again – his cigars. Then I had an idea: instead of going into his house, I'd just sit inside his car. On our way back from town the other day, I asked Dad to drive past his house. We saw that his car was still there. I wanted to get out and walk around, but Dad wouldn't stop. I knew his car was unlocked. David's car was *always* unlocked. And I knew that if no one cared enough to deal with his estate, no one thought to lock his car. I decided to wait on any plan until everyone was gone for the summer. I wanted to enjoy our last day on the lake together as a family. Sometimes, when things happen in life, we forget to count our blessings. It was a beautiful day on the lake. The family was together. The sun was shining and none of us were dying of cancer.

The following day came and Mark and Staci were packing the truck to drive back home. Mark and I hadn't talked any more about our conversation at the picnic table, though by this time I had decided that I was possibly not strong enough to go to David's house. Thoughts of walking over there made me anxious. I wondered if going over there was necessary. I gave myself pep talks – tried talking myself out of putting myself through that…sparing myself that experience. *There are enough experiences in life when we can't be spared*, I kept thinking. Still, a part of me wanted to go and see what I'd see. I wanted to find out if my anger was justifiable. I secretly couldn't wait to find out what I'd ultimately decide to do. Deena and Jess wouldn't be up for another week or so, so I had plenty of time to decide.

My decision, however, was made seventeen minutes (*one minute for each month David has been gone*) after Mark and Staci's departure when I received this text message from Mark's phone:

> DAVID'S CAR WAS UNLOCKED WITH THE KEYS ON THE SEAT. THERE WERE CIGAR PACKS ALL OVER. I GRABBED YOU ONE OF THE PACKS WITH A SINGLE CIGAR LEFT INSIDE. I LOVE YOU.

It was a cold, gloomy afternoon. Mark and Staci had arrived safely back home, and Dad and Robin were beginning to pack up their things for their journey home. Everyone was busy working like elves on their own "end of this year's vacation project." The unspoken was in the air, though. There was one thing left to do and the gray clouds looming overhead were our adamant reminder. The darkest most dismal afternoon of this year's vacation was perfect for the task Dad and I were about to perform.

It was ten minutes to two when I went into the lake to fetch the boat and bring it to the dock. The water was far too choppy for me to maneuver the dinghy, so Dad had me swim out to the pontoon boat and pull it in. The wind made it almost impossible for me to pull the boat, as it was blowing in the opposite direction from the dock.

The water felt like liquid ice. Between the plummet in body temperature from jumping in and the upset by this call of duty, my body trembled. I didn't want to go in the lake. I hadn't been in the lake all summer because David was in there. Thoughts of swimming in the water, at the bottom of which the remaining parts of David lie, paralyzed me. *I don't love the lake this summer.* I've never *not* loved the lake.

It's difficult for me to go back to that moment. I can't picture my bathing suit. I don't remember if Dad and I even spoke. I can just taste the tears that fall from my eyes as I write.

I didn't want to touch the box. Dad had set it in the corner on the back seat of the boat, near where the canopy had been folded. There was a pocket of rain from the pouch and it was dripping on the box. If I left it there, David would have gotten wet. If I moved it, I'd have to touch his remains. By that time, though, Dad was steering the boat toward the first stop, where he would soon instruct me to "Take one-quarter of the ashes and put them into the water." Reluctantly, but without appearing so, I picked up the box and placed it on the table in front of me. It was heavier than I thought it would be.

Once we were out front of the camp David grew up in, Dad put the boat in neutral, and I wondered what I would do in this moment of truth. I didn't want to touch the box, but the wind was picking up and the water was becoming choppier. Dad quickly pulled the boat out of neutral and told me to "do it now." He couldn't keep the boat in that spot for long.

I opened my hands to receive the box in front of me. I tried taking a deep breath, but a series of shallow inhalations was all I could muster. Earlier this day, in attempt to prepare myself for this adventure, I tried to imagine, for the first time in my life, what a cremated body looked like. I concluded that it must look like ashes from a cigarette, or a Swisher's Sweet, in David's case. (After all, they are called *ashes*.) A revolting mix of black and white. Ignobly grey. The salt and pepper that fell from the cancer stick.

I opened it to find a plastic bag full of what looked like broken pieces of coral. *How did David get in here? How did David go from David to this?* I've heard people talk about "spreading" or "sprinkling" ashes, but now that it was becoming obvious to me that the "spreading" or "sprinkling" of these ashes was my job, I didn't have much time for deliberation. Still, curbing the rate at which these thoughts spewed from my conscience proved impossible.

"Spread" ashes. I don't like the word. One spreads out a blanket to sit on or one spreads almond butter onto a slice of bread. I couldn't "spread" his ashes. I could, however, sprinkle them, I supposed, but I didn't want to. I sat there frozen with him on my lap. I held onto that box so desperate for David to come back. Desperate to wake from this terrible dream. I hugged him to my body and I began to shake. It was pouring now, but I held onto him with all my love, shielding him from the rain. Grandma, my maternal grandmother always said that when it rained it was because god was crying. Unsure of whether or not I believe in a god (or just afraid to admit that I don't), I imagined a god. Someone's god somewhere, in that moment, hurting for David in this box. Hurting for Dad, staring with such sadness in his eyes, at his best friend inside the box I clung to. Hurting for my family who missed him as much as I did. Hurting for myself. Yes, I imagined a god crying.

Then I started crying.

And the rain continued to pour from the sky and the tears continued to pour from my eyes. It was impossible to discern raindrops from teardrops. We were soaked to our cores and if I didn't do something quickly, David would have been, too. The pelting raindrops stung my face. I looked over at my dad in the driver's seat, but between the wind, the rain and the tears, I couldn't see him. I don't know if he was crying. I was glad it was raining. I wanted the rain to wash this day away.

How do I get these ashes from the box and into the water? I didn't want to touch the contents, but when Dad said again that it was time to take out one-quarter of the ashes, I knew I had to. I could have told him I couldn't bring myself to reach inside the bag, but I decided it was better for me to just do it. I didn't want to make it a production. If Dad had wanted to do it, he would have done it. (Or maybe he thought I wanted to?) It was time.

I did it. I didn't want to do it, but I did it.

I reached my cold, wet, trembling hand inside the plastic bag. Whites, off whites, with some pinkish and yellowy/brown mixed in. Ashes? Chunks! PIECES. I looked at my dad, aghast. Frozen. Horrified. Was I too old to be this naïve? I looked at him panic-stricken. Immobile.

"Bone," he said.

I don't know where the tears came from. I don't remember ever crying so hard, though I'm sure I have. When I grabbed the first handful of David, I threw up in my mouth and swallowed it. Chalk on my wet hands, sticking to my skin. I stood up and held onto the side railing with one hand and extended my other hand out over the water. Just as I began to relax my hand and open my fist, the wind turned and all of David in my grasp blew onto my sweats. Into my face. Down my neck. On my bare feet. The wind and the rough water rocked the boat and I almost fell. I took a heavy step backward to regain my balance and stepped on a piece of David which cut into my foot. I thought I would throw up again, but I didn't. I was careful not to inhale for fear of his cancer growing inside of me, but what if I did? Just to be sure, I coughed. I coughed hard. I induced a coughing fit until I again thought I would throw up. I didn't. But I coughed all night.

The next week, I had to drive to the post office to pick up a package that had been delivered for me. Gramp went for the ride with me, and on the way back, he told me to turn right out of the lot.

"Shouldn't I turn left? That's the way we came."

"Right," he said. So I turned right. "Go up the hill and take the road on the right. It looks like it leads to a cemetery."

A moment later, on our way up a hill, I saw a road on the right, but it actually was leading into a cemetery, so I wasn't going to turn until Gramp said, "Here. There's the road." Confused, I did what I was told.

"Take the second left," he said. "Follow it down and turn right when I tell you to." I took the second left and turned right when directed.

"Follow the bend right here and stop the truck."

We were in the middle of what I thought must have been one of the oldest cemeteries in New England. I couldn't imagine what we were doing there. David had been cremated, so we weren't visiting him. Were his parents buried here? Where *had* they been buried? That was a question I never thought to ask him. Luckily it wasn't too late, since he was sitting next to me and not beneath any of the headstones that surrounded us.

Staying in my truck, I looked around at some of the headstones. The names and dates were difficult to decipher on many of them, but others were clearly from the 1800s. So many of these people had lived and died before Gram and Gramp's parents were even born. It was a beautiful cemetery...if a cemetery can be beautiful. I looked at Gramp as if to say, "OK...Why are we here? I'm not getting it."

Without gesturing, he just looked at me and said, "It's on the left."

I turned my head to the left and looked out the window. Then I saw it. A pink headstone with Gram and Gramps' names on it:

Jesus.

I hadn't expected that. Immediately grateful, more so in that moment than ever before, that they were both alive and well, I scrambled for something to say. I knew it was important to both of them to purchase their headstone themselves. They have always felt strongly about not putting that monetary burden on the family...about being as independent and responsible as possible...about planning for their own funerals instead of avoiding the topic because, well let's face it, who wants to think about their own funeral? At that moment, I could only think of two things, both of which were stupid. *Um...it's pretty.* And *I'm glad you're not in it.*

I just wanted to get out of there. I wanted to get back to Stagedoor where Gram was waiting for us. I wanted the three of us to be together, all breathing under the same roof. Even if we didn't talk. I just wanted to know they were there because I realize they will not always be.

"Now you know where it is," he said.

I thought for a moment about the number of times that lie in my future when I'll visit them there. I envisioned myself lying on the grass above them, between them, my head propped in one hand, while the other traced their names on the pretty pink stone they purchased and had engraved a decade before they employed it. I saw myself talking to them like they could hear me. I brought with me their great-grandchildren so they could see how they've grown. I could see myself crying to them because when it comes to them I am selfish and the child in me hoped they'd live forever. I pictured missing them with an inconsolable despondency I will never be able to imagine until that day comes, when I will begin to miss them for the rest of my life.

Pulling myself out of my thoughts and back to real-time, I was happy to have Gramp next to me, driving back to Gram, all of us breathing. Alive. For another summer.

That night I lie in bed thinking about a heaven. I wished for a moment that I believed in a heaven like Gram does. When Grandma died, my six-year old self lay awake at night wondering why, if a heaven did exist, there wasn't a phone line that connected me to it. If Grandma really were in a heaven, where she was cancer-free and happy, where all was well and great, why could she not tell me so herself? I thought "heaven" was the most absurd notion I'd ever heard of. I decided then, though I wasn't able to articulate it as such until years later, that the idea of a heaven must be induced by peoples' own insecurities. People want to know that they're "going to a better place," but the truth is, no one knows what happens to us after we die because by the time we find out, we're already dead. By then, it's too late to report back. There aren't any phone lines.

I woke several hours later to my mind repeating *603.555.0722, 603.555.0722, 603.555.0722...* David's phone number.[2]

Gram and Gramp had gone to bed and the house was still in the night. I lie awake listening to the sounds of owls and other wild animals that only seem to come out while we sleep.

I got up to use the bathroom. The light inside Camp that was once left on for Mark and I when we came home from our late-night jaunts across the lake to Western Lake Shores, is now left on for Gram and Gramp. Its new purpose is to assist them in making their way out of bed to the bathroom and safely back without bumping into anything or, worse, falling.

603.555.0722...

Back on the porch, I crawled into bed under the warm covers and I listened to the quiet. A few years ago, Gramp started having terrible dreams. Night terrors. He doesn't have them often, and when he does, he doesn't remember them. The doctors say Gramp's night terrors are the beginning of Alzheimer's. Listening to him breath, I think: *In time we grow up. Then we grow old. If we're lucky.*

I lie in bed, eyes wide open, staring at the moon's reflection on the water. The trees, just a few feet away

---

[2] David's phone number has been changed to an invalid number.

from where I lie, carry the wind through the screened windows, where the breeze cuddles my hair and tickles my nose. It smells like home. I listen to Gramp's breath through the open window that separates their bedroom from the porch and adjust mine until we breathe in unison. Tonight, I will not allow myself to wonder how many summers I have left of being up here at Camp with Gram and Gramp. I will not allow myself to think about when they will take their last breaths. This is now and they are here. I can hear them.

603.555.0722...

Just to complete the experience, and for no other reason, I pick up my cell phone and dial David's number. It rings twice and then I hear a feminine computerized voice tell me, "The number [I] have reached 555.0722 in area code 603 is not in service." I am directed to "Please check the number and dial again."

I hang up and go back to my Address Book. *Gingham, David. 603.555.0722.* I have not misdialed.

I dial it again.

Same recording.

Right - there aren't any phone lines.

CHAPTER 8
An Evening with Jack Mann

~

In 2002, author David Collison flew in from England to interview Gramp for a book he was writing on sound design. He spent a few days with Gram and Gramp at their house in New Jersey discussing Gramp's work in the theatre. I never knew of Mr. Collison or of his trip.

As kids, Gramp would always tell us "You gotta have a project." If he ever saw us sitting down watching television or sleeping late, he'd tell us to turn off the TV and go read a book or get out of bed and go play outside. "You spend all this time rotting your brain with the television and dreaming about it when you could be learning something. Aren't there any books in the schoolhouse?"

Mark and I, along with our cousins Tara and Bob often felt discouraged by such comments. I believe I can speak for the four of us grandchildren when I say that, as kids, we often felt intimidated by Gramp, though I think in our hearts, we knew his words always came from a good place. He simply wanted us to grow into intelligent beings and to be successful at more than one thing. This made sense to me many years later when, as an adult, I asked him what characteristic he valued most about himself. Without hesitation, he replied, "Having tried for forty-five years to do my job better than anybody else. That's what we tried to teach our kids, and if you look at Brian and Kay, I guess we've done that." My dad is a logistics manager for a large corporation headquartered in Philadelphia and Aunt Kay is a self-employed Certified Registered Nurse First Assistant in surgeries in various hospitals in South Jersey.

Gramp has taught me to challenge myself. He has shown me that in doing so, I am more successful. "Sis, it isn't a challenge if it isn't a struggle, and if there isn't a struggle, there isn't a reward." Any advice from a man who, when asked if he could start his life over again, says he wouldn't change anything, is advice I'll welcome freely. "I was on vacation for forty-five years. What's to change?"

On the eve of my high school graduation, I asked Gramp to share a piece of advice with me. "Do your job better than anybody else," he said again, "and you'll be fine. You have to put forth an effort. You can't just coast.

My father told me that." I knew then, though not to the extent that I know now, that he listened. So I did, too.

If I believed it were possible for a person to be too smart for college, that person would be Gramp. He attended Flint Junior College for one year. During his time there, he earned barely passing marks. "I'm not a student. I'm a straight *D* student. My worst subject was Chemistry. I had a *D* but my teacher told me 'I'll give you a passing mark as long as you promise me you'll never ever go to school again.' HA! That's how bad my chemistry is. Otherwise he said he'd fail me."

My modest grandfather completely failed to mention the *A* he earned that year in Analytic Geometry. When I asked him about it, he chuckled, "HA! The next time I heard of that stuff was in *Tap Dance Kid*. There was a young man going to college at the same time he was in the show and every time I saw him he was reading his big thick book." I shake my head in amazement. If I had been lucky enough to earn even a *C* in Basic Geometry, I might have boasted it to the world. Not so humble am I.

One evening at Camp that summer, Gram and I were sitting on the porch. I had cooked, Gram washed, and Gramp was still drying the dishes. Gram and I chatted while we waited for Gramp to commence our evening chat together. When he joined us, he said, "All the things you should know, you absorb all by yourself without even knowing it. Your own character is formed by being around the people you're around. It's like being a trained dog. Whatever you do every day is your training. So when you're around people like your grandmother, whether you want to or not, you absorb some of her traits and that makes you some of what you are. So you're lucky that you've got someone like that around, instead of the obvious difference."

Gramp often says things that take a moment for me to process. Though there is a lesson in every word he produces, I am often left staring at him for a moment before I can formulate a response. Clearly, he wants to make sure that I know that we are all products of our environment. He, for some particular reason, is making sure that I am aware that if we surround ourselves with good and positive people, that energy will mirror itself in our own lives. Likewise, he feels it is necessary to intimate that the opposite is true.

Gramp didn't just say this to me on a whim. I know he thought about it the whole time he dried the dishes. Still, I wonder where this particular piece of advice came from and why it came on this night. Tonight, I will not ask. I am tired and I can tell it might agitate him. My impatience is derived from him (originally, perhaps, from his father), so I understand. Where the advice came from doesn't matter, anyway. It came to me from him, and so his advice will be taken.

The following February, Gram and Gramp received an e-mail from Mr. Collison informing them that his book had gone to print and that they would soon be receiving a personal copy for themselves. This was the first time I'd heard of Mr. Collison and his trip six years prior. The whole family couldn't wait to read what he had written about Gramp's work. We were excited to learn about him from someone who wasn't a member of our family.

A short time later, when I went to their house for a visit, Gramp greeted me with the book in his hands and a bright smile on his face. I took the book from him and opened it. In Mr. Collison's handwriting I saw:

Jack,

With gratitude for all your pioneering work and for being so kind to a struggling sound man in the 70s.

Best wishes,

David

Gramp looked at me and his beaming eyes said, "There's more, Sis." I turned the page and then I saw:

This book is dedicated to Jack Mann – one of the great pioneers of Sound Design.

Jack Mann is "one of the great pioneers of Sound Design." He is more than just mentioned in two books written by David Collison and the second book is dedicated to him. Jack Mann - my Gramp. No one ever told me. It wasn't until I really began doing research for this book that I started to learn just who my Gramp is.

In November 2008, about nine months after Mr. Collison's e-mail, Gramp received a personal letter from Carl Lefko - President of the United States Institute for Theatre Technology (USITT). The first part of the letter read:

Dear Mr. Mann,

On behalf of the USITT Board of Directors and the Awards & Resolutions Committee, we are pleased to congratulate you on being chosen to receive the USITT Distinguished Achievement Award in Sound. This award is given to honor an individual who has established a career record of achievement in his or her specialty.

On Friday, March 20, 2009, Dad, Mark, Staci, and I drove to the Duke Energy Convention Center in Cincinnati where we met Gram, Gramp, and Aunt Kay for a panel discussion with Gramp and Mr. Collison. The event was called *An Evening with Jack Mann.*

When we arrived at the hotel, Mark and Staci went to Gram and Gramp's room to get ready and Dad and I went to Aunt Kay's. We had exactly thirty minutes before we were all to meet downstairs at the bar to share a toast before heading to the convention hall. As I was getting out of the shower, I overheard Dad and Aunt Kay laughing and reminiscing about a time when she was in high school and she showed up at the theatre with a group of friends and Steve (Sondheim) said something to her that became a sort of nickname. Because we were in such a rush, there wasn't time to ask her to tell me the whole story. I can still hear the two of them laughing, sounding so happy and proud of their father.

From six o'clock until seven-fifteen that evening, Gramp talked about his work in the theatre. He told stories and answered questions from the audience. He made a room full of people laugh and, at times, he made some us cry. As I sat there and listened to Gramp, I couldn't ignore the phrase that echoed in my head, *A star is born*. Actually, though, the star we were all there to see, adoring fans that we are, was born almost eighty-six years ago. Thirty-seven years after his birth, he greeted the world of Broadway when he revolutionized theatre sound. Forty-eight years after that, he is still shining. He is still a star.

People flew in from all over the United States to listen to and to meet the renowned Jack Mann. We spoke to a few people who flew in from outside the U.S. as well.

When the panel discussion was over, they stood in line to shake hands with Gramp. Some students studying Sound Design in college waited for Gram and Gramp's autographs. People wanted their picture taken with them. When we had pictures taken of our family, some asked if they could jump in, while others snapped the same shots with their cameras. A few people asked me for copies of my thesis, upon its completion and encouraged me to take it even further by writing a book, assuring me they'd all buy a copy. I felt for a brief moment famous by association.

Taking a break from being photographed, I stood back and watched Gram and Gramp. Throughout the evening, I kept reminding myself to "be here and now" and to breathe it all in. To concentrate so I could remember. So I could tell the story. I watched my dad and Aunt Kay -- the proud children of this amazing couple one hundred and fifty people came to honor. I watched Mark who, like me, appeared overwhelmed with pride. Staci, beautiful soul, had the video camera on *record* the entire time. I looked at the faces of the strangers who knew more about my Gramp's career than I did. I listened intently to what they told all of us.

A professor from Purdue University told my dad that no matter where you go in the world, when you're talking about sound design, one hundred percent of the time it goes back to "How did Jack Mann do it?"

A sound designer from England told me that Jack Mann is the person whom she aspires to be "half as successful as" in her own career in designing sound.

A student from Susquehanna University told me that he hopes my family "...will remember what [Gramp] did for the world of Theatre for generations."

After the excitement of the discussion ended and we made it to our dinner reservation, one hour late, I turned to Gramp and asked, "Well, Famous Gramp, what do you have to say for yourself? How do you feel?"

"Famous," he smiled. Then he asked, appropriately so, "How was the sound?"

Sound designers were not presented with Tony Awards until 2007. Had they been awarded during Gramp's career, we were told in Cincinnati, he would have earned about eleven of them. I never knew any of this to the extent that it actually was...to the extent that it still is, until that evening.

Gramp has been retired from the theatre for twenty-three years, but his name still soars in Broadway history. His name has been printed in books all over the world; chapters have been devoted to his work; a book has been dedicated to him. In a note to him, Hal Prince referred to him as his "favorite sound genius." Stephen Sondheim used to call him "Genius Jack." He is admired and respected by all who have ever known him on a professional level or otherwise. He is a husband and father of two; grandfather of four, and great-grandfather of four. He is kind and loving, funny and serious. He is Broadway's first great American Sound Designer. He is Jack Mann. My Gramp.

CHAPTER 9
Curtain Call

~

One might find it ironic that a man who spent his life designing sound now wears two digitally programmed hearing aids. Gramp was never a particularly social person; he's always been more of a one-on-one conversationalist. Many people, outside of our family, do not know this about him. Though he was never what I would call the life of the party, he was always in the midst of it all at family gatherings. With Tara and Bob both married with children and Mark and Staci on their way to the same, our once small family has grown larger. Now, Gramp sits off by himself at our gatherings, often overwhelmed and sometimes dizzy from the noise around him.

Gramp has long-since stopped enjoying going to the theatre. "The sound is just terrible nowadays. It's all run by computers and it's too loud. Natural amplified sound was something else." Though my knowledge of the subject is scant compared to Gramp's, I think I understand what he's talking about. I feel similarly when it comes to photography. A photograph that has been electronically altered is not photography. There is little art form left in the field with digital cameras these days. The pictures themselves can look beautiful, flawless, but that doesn't make them *photography*. True art, in its raw form, is flawed. Two of the same cannot exist. So it also must be with "raw" sound. Actors' voices contain imperfections. If those sound imperfections are replaced with (computerized) perfect monologue and song, again, the art form is lost. And it cannot be Jack Mann sound.

When Helen Keller was asked which was worse, being blind or deaf, she said being deaf was worse because, "Blindness separates people from things; deafness separates people from people." Though, due to his age, Gramp is hard of hearing, not deaf, his hearing loss has become significant enough to separate him from people. As a Sign Language Interpreter who knows a good bit about hearing loss and the various causes, I understand him. Though it makes me sad because I miss him, I realize that he is probably just as sad and misses us more.

A lot has changed in our family since that night in Cincinnati. Just three weeks before Gramp was due to present there, he became very ill. He was hospitalized for a week and we almost lost him. Amazingly, he made a full recovery by the time they were due to fly out and we were all able to enjoy *An Evening with Jack Mann.*

Three months later, Aunt Kay received a far worse diagnosis. I wish with all my might that I could change the ending to her story. If this book were fiction, one must believe I would.

You lay stretched out on the loveseat. Your 5'11" stature looked so long atop that couch. Your limbs hung with grace. You rested there like a composed ballerina. That's how I always saw you when you walked, sat, or even just stood. Your right leg was piked straight out in front of you extending almost a foot beyond the armrest and your left leg was bent, with your knee leaning against the back of the couch. You wore your pink cap and soft white fleece top with equally comfortable looking pants. A blanket rested over your increasingly thinning body; you were warm and cozy. A rough copy of this manuscript rested on your lap, propped against your thigh. You struggled to turn the pages...your coordination was worsening. After a moment, a light sigh and a long smile confirmed to me, who sat on the longer couch next to you, that you had found the part you were looking for. You began to read, and I sat back and watched you with preponderant hesitation.

I wanted to tell you things...things I wanted you to know, but every time I thought about formulating those thoughts into spoken language, I pulled back. I thought that if I told you these things you'd think I only said them because you were so sick. And I thought that if I told you these things, it meant that I was acknowledging how sick you had become. I didn't want to acknowledge that because if I did, you might really become as ill as I feared you had. I *knew how sick you were, though. I just didn't want to admit it.* I hoped that by not admitting it, maybe it could be taken back. If I played dumb to the situation, maybe the situation itself would cease to exist. And you would be cured...or, even better, the doctors would realize they'd made a terrible mistake and diagnosed the wrong person. We'd learn that you were in fact fine and healthy and permitted to return to your normal, daily activities. Instead of going back to the hospital, you could go back *to your work* in the hospital.

I wanted to tell you that I had been thinking it was time to finish this book. I hesitated to tell you, though, because I knew that if I made that promise, I'd have to keep that promise. I hadn't felt much like writing lately, and for the first time ever, I didn't care. I knew it would take some devastation and healing before I was ready to sit down and face a blank page again. Why rush that? It had been almost six months since you were diagnosed with adenocarcinoma and I was still so dizzy with fear and busy bargaining with a god I really didn't think existed.

I stared at you as these thoughts raced, tirelessly, through my head. I had visions of all of us eager to forgive the doctors for misdiagnosing you. We chalked it up to "mistakes happen." We did not care because we had you back. You, the selfless daughter, sister, niece, wife, mother, aunt, grandmother, friend. You, the nurse, who had spent your career saving people's lives until it was someone else's turn to do the saving. But today, as I watched you, it seemed like the doctors were failing.

I wanted to tell you how much I loved summers at Camp with you the last five years. We had grown so close and it meant so much to me to have that relationship with you. I wanted to reminisce with you about our outlet shopping on those rainy New Hampshire days...about the time you took Andrea and I to Dragon Feathers for martinis, and then we had to shop for a few more hours because none of us could drive home...about the time we bailed all that water out of the quickly sinking Music Mann. We saved the boat that morning and I haven't gotten into it since then without remembering our teamwork. I never will.

I wanted to tell you how much I always loved your smile. Your smile was contagious. I didn't know which part of my work was making you smile like that. I didn't know what you were thinking. I didn't know how you were feeling. I didn't know if you even knew I was there or if you knew I was watching you. I didn't know how long you would stay there reading. It was two days after Christmas, and I didn't know that was the last time I would ever see you.

You left behind both of your parents, your husband of forty years, your two children, your four grandsons, your brother, aunts, uncles, cousins, nieces, and nephews. You left behind a list of friends so long I wouldn't even know where to hang it. You left behind a super-sized world filled with people who, almost six months ago, began missing you with desperate pain. We will never get over the loss of you, dear Aunt Kay. We will never try. We will, however, after enough time passes for each of us individually, come to terms with the reality of this loss and learn to let some of the hurt go, to cry less, to smile more (as you would want us to) and to celebrate you and the constant stream of life and love that you emitted.

I haven't been able to write much since you passed away. That burn that I'd always had in the depths of my soul...the burn that always seemed to write for me, was gone. For a while, I wondered if it was gone forever, and again, I didn't care. It's been six months since you've been gone, and though I never officially promised you that I'd finish this book, I'd be lying if I said you never made it clear how much you wanted me to. And so this morning, I decided it is time. Just like that. Right now. It is for you, my esteemed Aunt Kay, whom we all miss with dire sorrow, that I, at last, end this book.

Today is July 4, 2010. It is Jack's twelfth birthday and Stagedoor's seventy-second. In less than two weeks, Gram will celebrate her eighty-eighth birthday at Camp with Tara, Jack, Kevin, Brady, and our wonderful neighbors, The DeWhittney's. Two days after that, on July 19th, Aunt Kay would have been sixty-three years old. Gram and Gramp didn't go to Stagedoor last summer because Kay had just been diagnosed. They didn't want to leave her. They said they'd wait until this year when she was in remission and they'd go up together to celebrate their birthdays as they always did.

And so as the seventy-second year since Stagedoor was built is among us, we are facing the first year without Aunt Kay. There is an overwhelming amount of emotion we are all experiencing, but it feels like none of us has much to say. I expect that when we get up there we'll go through the motions, each of us separately and in our own way. We will all face challenges of our own in continuing to breathe through this process. We will continue to love and support one another, and somehow everyone will be alright. *In time everyone will be alright.* It's just so hard to see it that way now when we are all hurting so much.

We will all miss Aunt Kay at Camp this summer. We will always miss her. Some might miss her so much they can't bring themselves to make the trip up there. Others can't wait to get up there because that is where they can feel her strongest presence.

Kristin and I are leaving next week to spend a week at Camp. She hasn't met Stagedoor yet, but she has read an earlier draft of this manuscript, seen pictures, and listened to stories. She already loves Camp. I am not sure what to expect this time, though. I can't wait to introduce her to my special, safe place in my favorite corner of the world, but I am also concerned about how this year's trip will affect me. When it comes to matters of the heart, there isn't a soul on this planet who is weaker than I am. To make matters worse, I do not deal well with change…specifically, in this case, death.

Then there is David's house. I've gone by there every summer since he died. I spoke with Mrs. DeWhittney last week and asked about his place. Three and a half years later, his estate is still untouched. Some of the windows in the back have been boarded up because trespassers had apparently found their way inside. Everything else, I was told by another neighbor, remains the same. Spooky. Sad. I feel hatred toward his biological family, and I'd love to be there when karma gets all of them.

Tara has called twice to share with me some of the changes she's seen in Gram and Gramp since she's been with them this summer. As difficult as it is for us to observe these changes, what affects us even more is how Gram and Gramp respond to them. Because of the uneven ground, walking outside has become difficult for them. They can no longer sit under their favorite tree and look out at the lake. They can't walk down to the dock anymore or go for rides on our pontoon boat. These are just some of the things that they always loved to do.

Gram is still unbelievably independent, but I worry about her having to take care of so much on her own. She and Aunt Kay used to grocery shop and cook together; now, Gram is responsible for doing all of that on her own. Last year, Gramp's doctor advised him to stop driving, so Gram, after several decades of being a passenger, has taken his place behind the wheel. Old age creates challenges that they face on a daily basis, but with the constant, selfless support of their son-in-law Uncle Bob, their son, their four grandchildren, and the rest of the family, they deal with them together.

I am just grateful to have another summer up there with them. And I am grateful that Kristin will experience Camp with Gram and Gramp, too. Camp without Gram and

Gramp just won't be Camp to me. Not for a long time, if ever.

I imagine Camp to be quite still in Kay's absence. I close my eyes and I am standing at the end of Robin's trail, facing the lake. The air is stagnant. Thick. It is hot. I contract my abdominal muscles and expel as much air as I can through my nose and mouth simultaneously. I need to breathe like this to get the air circulating around me. We have to keep breathing so it can keep moving. We need to keep moving so we can keep living.

One day, Jack and Kevin will read this story and when Ben and Brady are a bit older, perhaps they will read it to them. I would love for Jack and Kevin to share their own stories with Ben and Brady and with all of the future children, when they come. They are the first great-grandchildren of Jack and Jean Mann and, with that, should come the honor of passing this torch. Gram and Gramp created the story. I wrote the story. Now Jack and Kevin can help pass it on.

On October 8, 2010, Gram and Gramp will celebrate sixty-eight years of marriage. I do not know how much more time Gram and Gramp have left on Earth in this life. I do not know how many more anniversaries they will commemorate together or if they will make it back to Stagedoor next summer. I do not know how many more times I will be able to say "I love you" and know that they hear me. I do not know how much more advice I will have the time to garner from them. I do know, however, that with the deaths of our friend David and our darling Kay, none of us are taking a moment for granted. Any of us can be next, so we must spend as much time with each other right now.

I know that with the impending reality of Gram and Gramp, we are aware, now more than ever, that we must continue to enjoy them until we are separated, and then, we have their story. The story *will not* end. Neither will yours, Aunt Kay. I am desperate for these words to find you: Time will not cause us to forget. I can still hear your voice. I can still see your beautiful smile and your sparkling eyes. They are so vivid that I don't even have to close my eyes to recall their detail. You have a part in every piece of Camp and inside every one of us. Time will *never* let us forget. I promise you.

Just as an actor cannot simply *play* the part, he has to *become* the part, so it is with writing. Consequently, in the last couple of years, the mere presence of Gram and Gramp has become a constant reminder that one day we will all be living our lives with only memories of them. I do not like to think about that. I cannot stand the thought of them ever not being here, yet I know one day it will happen. I am not in denial, but if I ever was, writing this book has certainly cured me of that. I am not in denial, but I don't have to think about it today. So I don't. I won't. Starting now.

Had I chosen not to finish this book, the children and future children of our family would have heard different stories – perhaps much like the stories I heard growing up. They would have heard the modest versions. Very different versions. I am indebted to Gram and Gramp for sharing with me all that they have. Without them, and without those who have come before us, this story would not be possible. Without them, this story would not exist. And without this bond founded by Eddie and Etta Wray that grows increasingly stronger with time, this story would not have had the adoration behind it to propel it into fruition.

This summer will be the strangest summer yet at Stagedoor. It will be the first of many strange summers, I am afraid. While I don't know exactly what to expect, I do know that if I've learned anything from my grandparents and those who have gone before us, it is that when the leads exit stage right, there's always something about to happen stage left. Their legacy will never die. Every year when we reunite at the lake, we will be reminded. Some years there will be fewer of us, and some years there will be more of us. Each year, we will re-experience the dream of our ancestors. As Aunt Kay so poignantly once wrote:

May all who visit this magical place, be it family or our special friends, share the beauty and happiness enjoyed through the years and the hope that its charm never ends.

Remember the dream of Aunt Kitty and Gramp (Eddie) that continues to inspire us all. A perpetual haven, our "Golden Pond" Camp, always ready for the next curtain call.

A spotlight shone directly in my eyes. It commanded every ounce of my attention. The light was so bright that I had to turn my head, for fear of my skin burning while I slept. The light overpowered everything I had ever felt before. I cared about nothing, no one, in that moment. I cared only about that light. It was so bright that I didn't need to wake from my dream to see it there. I was pulled toward it, just a touch…just enough before I forced myself to open my eyes and follow it to the end.

The moon. It is full tonight. I woke you twice to see the magic. I did not go back to sleep. As if moved by a force I could not determine, I seeped through the screen and stood at the edge of the dock. My body, being jerked with one snapping motion to the right, floated, now gracefully and effortlessly atop the water to the north end of the lake. My eyes followed two spotlights, transfixed, across from the mouth of the river where I made love to you that afternoon under the hot New Hampshire sun.

Unsure of how I got there, I closed my eyes and willed my now frozen self back through the screen and into bed…warm and cozy with you there.

I lie awake through the night and followed the moon across the lake. I chased the moon with you right there. I woke you a third time to borrow your camera, before realizing it had been left on the beach last night. Through the tiny holes in the screens, I spotted the Sea of Tranquility. I could almost see the Eagle landed there.

The sun began to rise. I closed my eyes to dream. I closed my eyes and I could see. I have willed you. Just like this.

Climb onto a rose petal and slide down the stem, to a world
no one knows of. No one but them…

Leap onto a rainbow and ride it across,
To the rocks in the stream and the lively green moss.

Ivy colored stone behind the waterfall, you can see…
Jump on in, take a swim – that's where you'll always find
me.

This place was created specially for us. It is easy to find.
Just close your eyes; I am never far behind.

We'll do cartwheels until we're dizzy, then we'll look up at
the sky,
Holding hands tightly and laughing until we cry.

We'll twirl in the moonlight and tumble through the weeds;
Follow a shooting star; we'll see where it leads.

You play the Princess and I'll play the Queen;
We'll dance with the fairies through the valleys of green.

We'll make the pinkie promise of a lifetime, napping
together on a cloud;
From now until forever, we will only dream out loud.

Where the sun meets the wind, that is where I'll be – right there with you, where our dreams run free.

At night when you sleep, I will meet you there. We'll eat chocolate kisses and pick daisies for our hair.

The birds sing for us as they fly and dance, too. Right there, it is true -- that's where I'll always find you.

Gram and Gramp about to return to
Stagedoor for the summer of 2010.

Made in the USA
Middletown, DE
23 June 2021